C000263294

"Another brilliant book from Alicia Eaton. Full of practical suggestions and common sense, this is a book for parents wishing to encourage their children to be well-rounded, independent thinkers."

**Lorrine Marer – Children's Behavioural Specialist
Channel 5's 'The Teen Tamer' and 'Families Behaving Badly'**

"This book will come as a huge relief to so many parents by helping them understand that much anxiety is actually part of everyday childhood worries and doesn't need to be catastrophised. Alicia Eaton gives so much practical advice with simple strategies that can be implemented immediately. Parents will feel calmer and their children will have a greater sense of wellbeing."

**Elaine Halligan – Director of The Parent
Practice Author of 'My Child's Different'**

"A comprehensive practical guide that will help children lead healthier, more productive and happier lives. A must read for every parent who has an interest in positive psychology and wishes their child to flourish with a growth mindset. Alicia Eaton delivers a masterpiece with clarity and sensitivity."

**Jason Pegler – CEO of mental health publisher Chimpmunka
Author of 'A Can of Madness'**

"In a world where there are so many anxious situations for kids, this book is invaluable. Working with students with learning differences, I see anxiety as the number one disrupter of behaviour and education. This book will help children develop invaluable lifelong skills, that are vital to everyone."

**Olive Hickmott – Learning Coach, Director of
Empowering Learning Author of 'Bridges to Success' and
'The Elephants in the Classroom'**

"*First Aid for your Child's Mind* is a great resource for every parent's bookshelf. In the 20 years I've been working with families and supporting parents with children's anger and anxiety related issues, this is the book I have been searching for. Clearly laid out and accessible, it gives comprehensive and helpful information so parents can support their anxious child more easily."

**Dan Jones – Hypnotherapist, Wellbeing Specialist: 'The Mind Changers'
Mental health awareness YouTuber and author of 'Relaxing Tales for Children'
and 'Sleepy Bedtime Tales'**

ALSO BY ALICIA EATON

WORDS THAT WORK: How to get kids to do almost anything

"Words that Work has some wonderful insights and I particularly love the chapter about the power and influence of your words on a child's life. A great read and I highly recommend that you grab your copy now."

Sue Atkins – ITV 'This Morning' Parenting Expert
Author of 'Parenting Made Easy'

"This is a very useful book for any parent of young children. Alicia will make you consider what you say and how you say it."

Felix Economakis – Counselling Psychologist: BBC's 'The
Panic Room'and 'Freaky Eaters' Author of 'Harden Up'

"Alicia has a real gift for communicating complex ideas in a way that makes them easy to incorporate into your daily routine. I highly recommend her work."

Michael Neill – Supercoach, Hay House radio host
Author of 'The Inside-Out Revolution' and 'Supercoach'

"If you have children this book will allow you to fully enjoy the wonderful experience of being a parent. Alicia has the gift of explaining complex psychology in an engaging and interesting manner."

Dr Stephen Simpson – Elite Mind Coach, Tedx Speaker
Best-selling author and Fellow of the Royal Society of Medicine

STOP BEDWETTING in 7 DAYS

"Stop Bedwetting in 7 Days is a very good book. I have found it to be clear, effective and have recommended it to a number of my patients."

Dr Anne Wright – Consultant Paediatrician,
Evelina Children's Hospital

"This book brings together the best of modern thinking and neurological development and I have no hesitation in recommending it."

Dr Mark Chambers – GP Trainer and
Integrated Healthcare Practitioner

"I have used this book with a number of patients and highly recommend this very effective method of treating this embarrassing problem."

Dr Jo Waddell – GP and NLP Trainer

FIRST AID FOR YOUR CHILD'S MIND

Simple steps to soothe anxiety, fears and worries

Alicia Eaton

Practical Inspiration
PUBLISHING

First published in Great Britain by
Practical Inspiration Publishing, 2019

© Alicia Eaton, 2019

The moral rights of the author have been asserted

ISBN 978-1-78860-117-7

The information contained in this book is intended to be educational and not for diagnosis, prescription or treatment of any kind of health disorder whatsoever. This information should not replace consultation with a competent health care professional should you be concerned about your child's mental health. The author and publisher are in no way liable for any misuse of the material.

 Practical Inspiration
PUBLISHING

I dedicate this book to the memory of my father Andrzej Olson (1930–2018) who showed us that it's possible to go through the worst of times and turn them into the best.

Acknowledgements

I've had the good fortune to meet and be trained by some of the wisest people on the planet and I thank them for sharing their wisdom and ideas. Because of them, I've been able to develop my practice and create programmes that have helped so many children overcome their problems and difficulties more easily. Paul McKenna is at the top of that list for 'changing my life' so I could go on to do the same for so many others; followed by Richard Bandler, co-creator of NLP; Michael Neill for his 'inside-out' thinking; Dr Roger Callahan for his creation of TFT (Thought Field Therapy); Dr Ronald Ruden and his brother Dr Steven Ruden for Havening Techniques; Olive Hickmott for her work with mental imagery in education; Dr Tom Barber and Dr Sandra Westland for teaching me about psychotherapy and hypnosis and also, the work of Dr Maria Montessori which continues to influence me greatly.

And thank you too, to the many friends and colleagues with whom it's always a pleasure to discuss ideas – I learn something new from every conversation however fleeting, in particular Toni McGuinness, Michele Paradise and Dr Stephen Simpson.

I thank too: Alison Jones of Practical Inspiration Publishing for her patience as I chopped and changed things around a thousand times, Liz Carrington for her artistic guidance and Emily Calnan for her book cover design.

Last but by no means least, the three shining lights in my life: George, Thomas and Clementine.

Contents

Introduction

We often hear that today's children are more stressed than previous generations. Growing up in an environment with worrying news items about the threat of terrorism or climate change, an endless stream of school exams and online social media bullying all contribute to a heightened sense of anxiety. Our new found 'connectivity' seems to have become a blessing and a curse.

Even when children are having fun playing computer games, their bodies produce an adrenaline rush that never quite gets burned off. These feelings of worry and 'generalised anxiety', as it's called, can quickly spill over into all areas of life.

I've been helping children in my Harley Street clinic overcome and manage feelings of anxiety for over 15 years, so I know the harsh and long-term consequences these can have if they're left unchecked. Anxiety can set back a young child's emotional growth and hamper performance in every area of their life. It will stop your child from making friends, taking part in social activities, sitting exams successfully and fulfilling their potential.

Ironically, worrying about a child's anxiety has become a major cause of stress for parents. Anxiety spreads through the home like an invisible gas – everyone can feel it but no-one's quite sure what it is. All we know is that 'it's catching'.

Each time an anxious child comes to see me, I see a little bit of myself in them, for I know what it's like to be a frightened child. I know what it's like to feel very, very scared. I know what it's like to hear voices and see shadowy figures in the dark corners of the bedroom when there's really no-one there. And to feel my heart pound so much I fear my chest might explode, for most of my childhood was spent like this – in a state of fear.

I was born Alicja Olszewska – the daughter of Polish refugees. My father lived in Warsaw throughout the Second World War and as a child he spent many years dodging bullets and hiding from Nazi soldiers. When the war was over, as a 16-year-old he was smuggled out of the country in the back of a lorry with his mother and brother. Arriving in England, they were reunited with my grandfather, a Polish RAF officer who also worked for the Polish Government in Exile in London. As a result, he knew he could never return to Poland and so the family were lucky they could be reunited here.

My father always said that by rights, he should have been killed many times over. Almost every day, he found himself in life-threatening situations and yet somehow managed to survive. He often wondered how and why he became one of the lucky ones and when I look at the devastation caused in that city by the war, I too am astonished. His family's home still stands there today and a neighbouring house bears bullet hole scars.

By contrast, my childhood in a London suburb was a very safe existence and yet what we now know to be my father's Post-Traumatic Stress Disorder dominated not only his life but also ours.

He would regularly wake up in the middle of the night with nightmares, screaming *"the soldiers are coming!"* Our kitchen cupboards were stuffed full of packets of rice, pasta, sugar and flour – war provisions, just in case. My father would get angry if supplies got too low – we would thank him one day, he said, when war came and people were starving. We also kept gas masks in the loft . . . *"just in case"*.

I remember the day when he went to the bank and exchanged some of his savings for Kruggerands. *"Gold will be the currency of the day when war comes"*, he would say. A piece of gold could save your life, for it would buy you the loaf of bread that would make the difference between living and dying. He dug a big hole at the bottom of the garden under the oak tree and buried all the gold coins there.

Despite being the son of an Air Force officer and having grown up on an air base, he had an intense fear of flying and never set foot in an aeroplane. As the years passed, he'd still be furious if he found out I was heading off on a foreign holiday that involved a flight for he always worried about us. Paradoxically, he loved watching air displays and collected model Spitfires too – but would automatically duck if he heard a noisy plane fly overhead.

My mother's childhood was equally traumatic with episodes of living in labour camps in Siberia, and so living on 'high alert' became a normal way of being for my family.

As children, my sisters and I were never taken to swimming pools – they were to be avoided at all costs for *"water is really, really dangerous"*. We were not allowed to own or ride bicycles – for you could fall off and *"kill yourself!"* And if *you* didn't kill yourself, then a passing car certainly would!

When I was 5 years old, I developed a phobia of dogs. A friendly Labrador jumped up at me on a family trip to the seaside. In his exuberance, the dog scratched my legs. Seeing drops of blood appear on my thigh, I panicked and started to run – and the dog duly chased me. It didn't matter how fast I ran, he ran faster. I couldn't get away from his hot breath and the sound of his panting over my shoulder. And the more I screamed, the louder he barked.

It took me over 30 years to control the feelings of panic that I experienced each time I came close to a dog.

Back in the 1970s when I was growing up, it was usual to let dogs roam freely on the streets, so a short 15-minute walk to school could take me up to an hour as I walked in a peculiar zig-zag fashion, crossing the road each time I saw a dog approaching. Also in the 1970s, terrorist bombs were regularly planted around London so we were warned by my mother never to walk near a letter box *"in case it exploded!"* This made the walk to school even longer.

So, I know fear. I know nightmares. I know the feeling of panic, for this is what I grew up with. 'Scaredy-cat' was my nickname. I know how debilitating it is and how it shrinks people's lives.

My anxiety remained with me right through to adulthood and rather inconveniently I also acquired a fear of travelling in lifts and on the London Underground – not helpful when you need to get to work on time. Oh, and I became scared of the dark too . . . and of flying in planes (of course – my father told me to be) and of spiders . . . well, you get the gist.

Fear is a strange and unusual emotion. Despite battling with life-long PTSD, my father was not a shrinking violet. He was a larger than life character who wanted to live every moment to the full, something he learned during the war. After all, you never knew when your life might end so you had to live every day as if it were your last. And for a man who could so easily panic and scream at the sight of a spider in the corner of a room, he had no fear when it came to running his business – a large and very successful electronics company. People often wondered if he'd simply been 'lucky', but we knew the real reason for his success was that he was prepared to take the kind of risks that most people would shy away from. He certainly *felt* lucky – after all, how else could he have dodged all those bullets and bombs – and in a strange way, his fear propelled him to achieve great things. He didn't stop running his business full-time until the age of 86.

When I began my training in clinical hypnotherapy and Neuro-Linguistic Programming, I started to understand how fears, phobias and anxieties are formed – and more importantly, how to get rid of them. I was fascinated to discover that it's actually possible to eliminate a fear or phobia of a spider or snake in just one day. Learning how to control the physical responses in the body meant someone who'd spent a lifetime screaming at the sight of a harmless house spider could learn how to stroke a tarantula or hug a python a few hours later and actually feel good about it.

As a mother of three now grown-up children, I know how much parents hate the idea of passing on their fears and anxieties to the next generation. We naturally feel we should be the strong ones protecting our young, raising them to be confident and brave. We want our kids to grow into self-assured, happy and successful people – we don't want them to grow up to be scaredy-cats like us. We want better than that for them, don't we?

With many years of experience in clinical practice now, I know just how common it is for adults to bottle up their own fears and try to keep them secret from their children. It's not unusual for existing fears and phobias to magnify once you become a parent, for that's the moment when you start to realise that you might just have to do something about your own anxiety – you'll need to *"face your fear"* or risk passing it on. And that is a scary thought, isn't it?

The first thing parents often say when they bring their child to see me is *"**I'm really scared** that I might be passing my anxiety on"*, without realising that simply by saying that within earshot, they've done just that. The words and language that we use around our kids can programme a young child's subconscious mind – just as my parents' did mine.

I still thank my lucky stars that I came across the world of NLP and hypnotherapy, which helped me shed my anxiety and learn how to breathe more easily.

I've now become passionate about helping others learn how to do the same and in this book, I'm going to show you how you can help your child get over their fears, phobias and anxieties . . . and (whisper it) *how you can get over yours* too. With a better understanding of how and why our minds create feelings of anxiety and an insight into the most effective way of handling this, you'll see how much easier and calmer life can become.

In this book you'll learn:

- the difference between a fear, a phobia and an anxiety;

- how words and language affect our thinking, feeling and behaving;

- what to say and what not to say to an anxious child;

- how the latest discoveries in the field of neuro-science can help us gain control; and

- cutting-edge psychological techniques and therapies for solving anxiety.

Take it from me, anxiety disorders are very treatable conditions. All of us can learn how to help children see that most feelings of fear and anxiety are just that – feelings. And the good thing about feelings is that they can easily be changed.

SECTION ONE

MAKING SENSE OF IT ALL

1

Anxiety

What's it all about?

The number of children seeking help for anxiety and mental health issues has risen sharply, recent data from the NSPCC's Childline service has suggested. Even those as young as 4 years old are said to be displaying signs of panic attacks, eating disorders, anxiety and depression.

In the last three years alone, 120,000 referrals were made by schools seeking professional mental health help with 56% of these referrals coming from primary schools, meaning an average of 183 referrals were made per school day in 2017/18.[1]

Experts blame the increase in school exams, the social media pressure to look good and appear popular, as well as family break-ups and worries about money. Coupled with this, we're now a 24-hour news society with an endless stream of information filtering into our homes. So whether it's a random terrorist attack on a city centre bridge or a tourist filled beach, a suicide bomber striking at a pop concert for teenagers, or an out of control wild fire, it's becoming increasingly hard to protect our children from hearing and seeing all the gruesome details.

It's often when these most tragic of events occur that we feel our most ill-equipped at explaining stressful events to children. Should we shield them from such horrors, or talk openly about them? And how can we help children make sense of such tragedies when we can barely make sense of them ourselves?

It's hardly surprising that anxiety levels amongst children have rapidly increased but ironically, worrying about their child's anxiety is one of the most common reasons parents give for having sleepless nights themselves. Even when kids are having 'fun' sitting indoors playing computer games, their bodies produce an adrenaline rush that never quite gets burned off. These feelings of worry and 'generalised anxiety', to give it its' proper name, can quickly spill over into other areas of life.

THE DIFFERENCE BETWEEN ANXIETY AND FEAR

Anxiety is the feeling that we experience in the lead up to a stressful event – in other words, it's our response to something that hasn't happened yet. How severe our anxiety becomes depends very much on our thoughts – we can make it worse just by over-thinking or dreading upcoming situations. Most of us will agree that we can exhaust ourselves with worry for no good reason – the reality often turns out to be a lot better than we predicted in our imagination.

Fear, on the other hand, is the emotion that we experience when we're actually in a dangerous situation. You may have heard of the 'fight or flight response' – it's our body's automatic nervous system response and it releases hormones from the adrenal glands such as adrenaline and noradrenaline. These will stimulate your heart rate, blood pressure and breathing rate and will give you that much required boost of energy to deal with the threat or danger. This is great if you really are in danger and need to run away fast, but our bodies haven't evolved to tell the difference between an attack by a grizzly bear and the more benign threats we'll encounter in a busy supermarket, on the road in a traffic jam or even the make-believe ones we'll see on TV or in computer games.

It can take up to 60 minutes for the effects of this automatic response to calm down and if these chemicals are not required, then they start to build up in our system and can have a draining effect on us. Not only will they have harmful effects on the body but we'll also start to feel as if we're 'on alert' and these physical feelings will trigger off yet more anxious thoughts. The mind understandably, will start to think there must be some good reason why the physical stress response has kicked in and if there isn't, will invent one for you with a sequence of anxious thoughts about events in the future.

And so the cycle will continue – your anxious thoughts will once again stimulate the automatic fear response and the stress chemicals released will get your mind wondering what's up.

The good news is that anxiety is a very treatable condition. Enlightened psychologists will now refer to anxiety as something that's often the result of an emotional *'injury'* to the mind rather than a 'disorder' – for that word immediately suggests it's part of a long-term problem and something to 'suffer'. In reality, it's now possible to heal an emotional wound rather than leaving it to fester and turn into something much bigger.

So, just as our children acquire bumps and scrapes on the outside of their bodies, we shouldn't be surprised to discover it's possible to get a few on the inside too.

We've become used to taking care of our physical health – think back to the last time you fell ill with an unexplained tummy upset for example, or sprained an ankle. The first thing most of us do is consult the internet and it makes sense to do this for we know we'll find useful advice there that will help us feel better faster.

However, when it comes to caring for our mental health it's a different story. As a society we shy away from talking about 'matters of the mind', feeling that the best way to deal with these is by adopting a stiff upper lip or leaving them to the professionals – but even then, we're not too sure what type of professional might be the right one for us. This fear of dabbling leaves far too many of us limping through life struggling with anxiety attacks or phobias that restrict us in so many ways.

Living with feelings of anxiety can have harsh and long-term consequences, and children can 'grow into' their fears rather than out of them. Anxiety can set back a child's emotional growth and hamper performance in every area of their life. It will stop your child from making friends, taking part in social activities, sitting exams successfully and fulfilling their potential. To make matters worse, those who suffer from anxiety and depression as children are likely to carry the problems into adulthood.

The feelings of stress and anxiety can manifest themselves in many different ways:

- an increase in cravings for sweet foods and snacks
- a reluctance to go to social events or visit friends' houses
- struggles with school work and lower grades
- inability to concentrate or follow instructions
- deafness or ringing in the ears
- persistent worrying with endless questions that have no right answer
- nightmares and difficulty in falling asleep
- bedwetting
- thumb-sucking, nail-biting, tics and stammers
- irritability and short-temperedness
- angry outbursts and sibling fights

Most parents will readily admit that when it comes to helping children deal with feelings of anxiety and worry, they feel inadequately prepared and quite simply 'lost for words'. It's not surprising, after all:

- What is the best way to explain news reports about terrorist attacks and bombings without alarming your child?
- What should you say to a child that's witnessed a tower block fire or disaster on TV and is suffering from nightmares as a result?
- How *do* you handle a child that's petrified of dentists, injections, dogs, spiders or even eating vegetables?
- Or help the child who is convinced the only thing they 'know' for sure is that they'll forget everything the minute they step into in an exam room?

HINT: It's not by saying *"Don't worry"*.

In order to develop into fully grown adults, children go through a process known as 'adaptation'. This is what gives human beings the advantage over animals – we have the ability to adapt to our environment precisely because we're not fully formed at birth and we take our time to develop into adults. If you pick up a newly born giraffe and stick him at the North Pole, he won't survive for very long for the possibility of growing a shaggy warm coat is not open to him.

Pick up a human baby on the other hand and transfer them from the UK to Japan and within a few short years they'll quickly become fluent in Japanese with no trace of an accent whatsoever. That baby has the ability to adapt to its' surroundings.

Your child's mind is open and ready to receive everything that's put in their path. In fact, it could be said that your child is in a state of 'waking hypnosis' – and you, as the parent, are programming that mind with all the things that you say and do.

This process of 'adaptation' is very powerful – a young child is using their environment to develop and in so doing, become a part of that environment. In a completely unconscious manner, children absorb the culture of their time and place along with the aspirations and attitudes of a society, simply by living in it.

Years ago, that process was very much simpler because life was more straight-forward. It is much harder for a child to adapt when their environmental influences are global rather than local, largely due to the internet.

Increased choices and chances offer today's children the kind of opportunities that can change lives. *"You can be whoever you want to be"*, our children are told – but who is that exactly? *"Reach for the stars and live the dream."* is a great motivational thought but with it can come a sense of endless inadequacy.

A primary school teacher recently told me that all the children in her class either wanted to be a 'YouTuber' or a footballer when they grow up. As they regularly read about teenagers becoming billionaires overnight, it's hardly surprising. *"Do think of a 'plan B' just in case"*, she told them.

There is a reason why so few people have an Olympic gold medal or an Oscar – they're not that easy to get hold of. So while I'm all for inspiring our children to have self-belief and become the very best version of themselves, growing up in a society that's constantly measuring success against those few, very outstanding people – or those with model-like looks and bodies to match – can only fuel anxiety and create a sense of disappointment.

Living a 'good' life with friends, family, regular work and a couple of interesting hobbies may sound a bit hum-drum but it's the kind of life that suits most of us and often is the key to happiness.

Today's children may have more choices and chances than ever before, but inadvertently this has turned into a poisoned chalice with the competition becoming ever more frenzied as the community they're growing up in is on the World Wide Web.

A couple of generations ago, a family would hand down not only their traditions and religious beliefs to a new child but also skills to prepare them for the world of work, which in all probability was going to be the same as that of their parents and grand-parents. Social mobility was not a thing discussed very often – your life was pretty much mapped out from the day you were born. I am sure none of us would wish to return to those days, but when you compare that world of certainty to the ever-changing environment that today's children struggle to navigate, it's not surprising that anxiety is so common.

How can you be sure of who and what you are when offered such an array of options and moral questions? Should you stop eating meat, for example, and become a vegetarian or better still, vegan? Will it stop global warming or is it too late? I regularly hear children being told that their generation needs to be the one that finds the solution to the climate change problem or the world will come to an end – no pressure there, then! They see their friends questioning their sexuality and even their gender and begin to wonder if they should do the same. With this ever-changing landscape it's no wonder so many children struggle to feel comfortable 'in their own skin'.

Back in the 1970s there were only three TV channels available so it's not surprising to learn that 30 million people sat down to watch a Christmas Day episode of *The Morecambe and Wise Show* in 1976. In those days, the shops were closed, churches were open, everyone watched the Queen's Speech and had roast turkey for lunch. That type of connectedness would be almost impossible to create nowadays, for even when families are all in the same house, they'll be living separate lives in different rooms.

Most of us would agree that too much choice is a hindrance rather than a help. I carried out a quick survey in my local supermarket and was shocked to discover there were 255 different types of tea on the shelves. That was just the tea section – I didn't count the coffee! Gone are the days when you were simply asked if you wanted tea or coffee, with or without.

As I moved into the aisle selling cleaning products and toilet rolls, the various combinations and permutations of special offers bemused me – should I have three packs for the price of two, an extra large pack with 25% off or go for the special offer with £2 discount? It's enough to frazzle your brain and the reason why we regularly see episodes of 'trolley rage' at the checkouts.

Too much information and too many choices lead to indecision and … anxiety. Remember, when our brain detects stress or a threat, that *'flight or fight'* response will be activated. The sudden quick release of chemicals might provide the burst of energy needed to jump out of the way of an oncoming car, but placed on 'high-alert' your brain will struggle to concentrate on smaller things. Contestants on TV quiz shows demonstrate this perfectly, as they struggle to answer the simplest of questions when the neuro-chemical overload makes their mind go blank.

***

Over the years, I've seen hundreds of children in my Harley Street clinic suffering from a huge variety of problems: fear of toilets, spiders and sharks, exam stress, strange obsessional thoughts, recurring nightmares, stage fright and nervous habits and tics. And it's no less varied for adults as I've worked with people who have phobias of big plants, zips and bananas.

As random as these problems may appear, they all have something in common. There's a structure and pattern to the way that our mind and body processes feelings of anxiety and creates those automatic fear responses.

While we may not always understand how someone could be so scared of something so seemingly trivial, it's important to accept that 'thinking about it' is creating genuine feelings. The structure and mechanics of the thought process are what produce the physical feelings of fear and anxiety, rather than the object itself.

In my clinical work, I use a blend of techniques from the fields of Positive Psychology, CBT (Cognitive Behavioural Therapy), mindfulness, psycho-sensory therapies, hypnotherapy and NLP (Neuro-Linguistic Programming). In this book, I'm going to explain what it is I do to help people overcome their fears and anxiety.

Armed with this information, you'll be able to adopt my strategies and techniques to keep your child in a calmer, happier, more resilient state able to face the stresses of everyday life more easily. Even just changing the words and language that you use on a daily basis, can change the way your child feels about themselves. And as every parent knows, when your child feels happy you'll feel happier and more relaxed too.

2

How your child's mind works

In this chapter, I'm going to give you an insight into how the mind receives and processes information and how this then becomes our thoughts, which in turn create the feelings that have an impact on our behaviour. As you'll see, having this knowledge will help you to address anxiety symptoms in your child more confidently.

A young child's senses are in a developmental phase for at least the first six years of life and during this time, it's not uncommon to see some children struggle to deal with the sensory overload. New tastes and smells can trigger a violent dislike of certain foods while for some, loud noises and crowded places will be difficult to handle. Some children hate the feeling of an 'itchy' shirt collar or a sock that continually slips down a leg, while others will be completely oblivious to the fact their clothes are a mess or they're covered in mud.

It's estimated that our nervous system receives around two million bits of information about what is happening around us, every second of the day. With so much information bombarding our minds, we have no choice but to filter or condense it down and make what are referred to as **deletions**, **distortions** and **generalisations,** like so:

Deletions: We automatically have to delete some of the information that we receive because there's simply too much of it so we *chunk it down* into a more manageable size. Because this can be a fairly random process, it's possible to throw away vital pieces of information without realising it. It's the reason why it's not uncommon to hear people arguing about the content of past conversations – one of them will insist that they did indeed say something and the other will claim to have heard no such thing. More often than not, both of them will be correct.

Distortions: We can make things seem better or worse than they really are as we make the information we receive compatible with our perceptions. In other words, it's not uncommon for our minds to have an idea and then seek out evidence to support it. For example: if you *feel* there are a lot of red cars on the road, it's very likely that red cars will 'pop out' at you as you drive along, supporting the notion. If you 'know' the party you'll be attending this evening is going to be dull, then it's very likely to be just that. Unconsciously you'll be seeking out proof to support this notion and only notice the negative aspects of it.

Generalisations: So that we don't have to relearn something every time we do it, our minds make *generalisations* to speed things up for us. For example, once you've learnt how to ride a bike, you can transfer that skill to every bike you encounter in the future, for they pretty much all work in the same way. You won't have to start from scratch trying to figure it out all over again. This is a very useful shortcut but this process of 'generalising' can cause problems too – for example, it will help you to develop a phobia of *all* dogs simply because you had a nasty encounter with just one.

This shrunken-down piece of information (after you've deleted, distorted and generalised) becomes what's known as your **internal representation**.

What then gets added to this cocktail of sensory information is the individual 'spin' we'll each put on what we're thinking. This spin will vary enormously depending on our **beliefs**, **values** and **past experiences**. We all have different influences in our lives so it's not surprising that two people can be in the same place at the same time and come away with a different version of the 'truth'.

Police officers see this happening all the time when taking witness statements. Five people may have witnessed the same traffic accident but they'll each have a different story to tell. This 'distortion' will, in all probability, come about innocently. For example, if one of the witnesses was themselves involved in a traffic accident just one week earlier and still feels a little shaken by it, then their perception of this new accident will be distorted. Perhaps they'll report that one of the drivers was driving much faster than they really were. It will simply have seemed as if they were to this particular person – for understandable reasons.

It's also why two people can come away from a cinema and one of them will declare the film to have been 'boring tosh' and the other one will think it's the best movie they've ever seen.

We each have a different version of the 'truth' – as I'm sure you've noticed on many occasions!

The two million bits of information that our nervous system gets bombarded with each second of the day get absorbed through our five senses: sight (visual), hearing (auditory), touch (kinaesthetic), smell (olfactory) and taste (gustatory), and we then turn that information into our thoughts.

Most emphasis is placed on the visual, auditory and kinaesthetic senses since they're the ones that we rely on most throughout the day. Our thoughts are mainly a combination of pictures, sounds and feelings.

1. VISUAL: OUR MENTAL IMAGES

As well as actually seeing the things around us through our eyes, we also create pictures or mental images inside our mind. As we think and speak we're constantly making images but they can flash through our mind so quickly that we may not even notice them.

Exercise

Read the following questions and take a few moments to think about each one before answering. Describe your answer out loud or write it down to make this process more effective.

1. What did you eat for breakfast this morning?

2. What's the capital of France?

3. Where is your dream holiday destination?

4. Who was the last person you called on your mobile phone?

5. What do you plan to eat for your next meal?

Some of you will have seen pictures as you thought about your responses, but others of you might have seen a word. For example, you may have seen the Eiffel Tower, the French flag or a croissant in response to the second question. Some of you will perhaps have seen the actual word 'Paris' and it may have been in colour or black and white.

Our mental images have an enormous effect not only on our feelings but also on our behaviour and the results we get. It's as if our bodies take these images as an instruction of what to do next. It's as if we are magnetically drawn towards getting what we see in our minds.

Understanding this is so important, since these images control our feelings of fear. A study carried out in America showed that a staggering 87% of people have a fear of 'something' lurking under the bed and refuse to sleep with their feet outside the covers for fear of being eaten up.[2]

I wonder how many of those people regularly check under the bed before climbing into it . . . just in case. Simply knowing (and looking for proof and evidence) that there is nothing under the bed is not enough to allay people's fears. When our imagination creates scary pictures in our mind, our body starts to respond as if those images were real. We can't tell the difference between a real or imagined experience.

Think back to the last time you watched a scary movie at the cinema or on TV. Even when you know for certain that it's make-believe, it won't stop you from having palpitations, sweaty palms and waves of anxiety in your tummy. Some of you will even scream out loud. This happens automatically in response to the images that you're seeing on the screen.

Becoming aware of the images inside your mind and learning how to control them, can help you to manage feelings of anxiety.

ACCESSING IMAGES

I know that some people will insist that they can't see pictures in their imagination but this affects only a tiny proportion of the population. The overwhelming majority of us do and it's just that we're not used to accessing them.

It's useful to help children become aware of their mental images as this can help with school work – reading and spelling in particular. I often tell children that it's a little like learning how to do 'silent reading'. When we first learn how to read, we begin by sounding the letters and words out loud. We'll continue to read out loud until around the age of six when quite often a teacher will ask us to start reading 'silently'. I can still remember being asked to do that and it seemed so strange to be told to read 'inside your head'. I didn't think it was possible, until I got the hang of it. And in the same way, we can teach our children to become aware of their mental images and practice playing around with them.

Enlightened psychologists now suggest that young school children be given lessons in mental imagery, especially those who struggle with dyslexia. When we spell words out loud, what we actually do is 'see' the word in our imagination first and then read it out loud.

Test this out with the word 'helicopter':

- Look away and slowly spell it out loud.

- Now spell it out loud again, but this time backwards.

Spelling it backwards might seem harder to do, but once you become aware that you're seeing the word in your mental image, then it becomes no more difficult than spelling it forwards – because what you're actually doing is *reading* it.

Some children need to 'see' a long way out in front of them in order to be able to access their images so it can help to look out of a window to do this. If your child struggles with school work, you may find it helps to ensure that their desk or table is not positioned right up against a wall.

A familiar phrase from your own childhood might be: *"Don't keep looking up at the ceiling – the answer's not up there!"* Teachers often say this to their pupils and yet, they're wrong. The answer is very likely to be 'up there' and I would recommend encouraging your child to look at the ceiling if they're struggling to figure out a problem to see if that would help. Looking down at a flat piece of paper on the desk shrinks the 'depth of vision' and certainly won't encourage the creative juices to start flowing.

To see this process in action more closely, watch the contestants' faces on a TV quiz show. As they're thinking of the correct answers, they'll be looking up. It could be to the left side or it could be to the right side depending on which part of the brain they're retrieving the information from. Some will look high up to the ceiling.

Perhaps you've noticed this in your own behaviour whenever you're put on the spot and asked to give your children's dates of birth, your address or telephone number. Most of us will automatically look out ahead and maybe slightly up too. The information isn't 'out there', but it 'feels' as if it is.

2. AUDITORY: OUR INTERNAL DIALOGUE

Not only do we have images passing through our mind all day, we're also hearing a variety of sounds. You might be hearing a piece of music – your favourite song perhaps, or it could be your own voice as it 'tells' you what you need to buy from the shops on the way home from work. Or it could be someone else's voice – how many of us have old arguments replaying through our mind, for example? Or it could be a complimentary voice – so much better to keep this one in mind.

It's not unusual for people to completely lose touch with their internal dialogue, as in the busyness of life it can go unnoticed. Stop for a moment now and silently ask yourself *"Where is my internal dialogue?"* and you'll locate yours.

In fact, we have a variety of inner voices – there's an upbeat, positive, happy one and a miserable, negative one too isn't there? There's one or even a few that don't sound anything like you at all – because they sound like other people. Your mother or father perhaps, a critical teacher from schooldays gone by – a whole cast of extras living inside your head, just longing to have a conversation with you, or tell you what to do.

Sounds and voices add to the drama going on inside our head and help to fuel those feelings of anxiety. Take a look at these sentences:

- *What's that funny noise?*

- *Did you hear that?*

- *I think I heard something shuffling around in the wardrobe.*

- *I'm sure I heard someone crying outside.*

- *I just heard footsteps – I think someone's walking around upstairs.*

How many of us would feel spooked sitting round a bonfire listening to ghost stories? You don't always need to be prompted by images to experience feelings of fear, as what you hear – be they random noises or words, such as someone's storytelling – will do the trick nicely. It won't take long for your mind to quickly conjure up some scary images to go with the dialogue.

For this reason, I'll also be teaching you how to take control of the sounds inside your head.

3. KINAESTHETIC: OUR PHYSICAL FEELINGS

Think about all the sensations and feelings we experience when we're anxious. You might have butterflies or knots in your tummy, a tingling in your hands or feet, a racing heartbeat and your legs might feel wobbly as if turning to jelly. Feelings can travel in waves from the top of the body down to the toes or in reverse, from the toes upwards. Some people will experience a pressure on either side of the head or a tightness in the chest making it difficult to breathe easily.

The human body has the ability to *habituate* – after time our response to a stimulus decreases. Imagine jumping into a cold swimming pool – yikes, it can be a horrible experience in the initial instance, but after a short while your body habituates to the temperature and then you simply stop noticing it, don't you?

It would be the same if I stamped repeatedly on your foot – it would hurt! But if I stood on your toes and kept completely still, after a few moments, you'd stop feeling pain.

This helps us to understand that when we experience physical feelings of anxiety for any length of time, they must be moving around or changing slightly. We know they're not static – because if they were, we'd quickly habituate and stop noticing them.

Becoming aware of specifically where inside your body you're feeling these unwanted sensations and the direction in which they're travelling, will enable you to change them.

SECTION TWO

STEPS TO SUCCESS

3

Detox your environment

As I mentioned at the start of this book, anxiety can be catching – it can waft around the house like an invisible gas affecting all who walk in its path. No-one needs to say anything but everyone can sense when something is not quite right.

While it's good to talk, I know that it's not always easy to get an anxious child to verbalise their thoughts. Younger children may not have the vocabulary or the self-awareness to identify their feelings and older children, especially teenagers, may not wish to admit to their fears or engage with you.

However, there are positive steps you can take to create a more calming environment for the whole family without the need to tell anyone – and here are a few suggestions:

CLEAR THE CLUTTER

An untidy house means you'll struggle to find things and always be in a rush or late. You'll get cross and stressed and so will your kids. Get a system in place – put hooks up on the wall and colour code storage boxes and shelves. Spend some time teaching your children where things will belong from now on. Have a 'lost property' box – go around the house picking up clutter and putting it in the box on a regular basis. When your child loses things, they'll quickly learn the logic in having a place for everything.

To help your child keep their bedroom tidy, I recommend taking a photograph of the room when it is at its' tidiest and sticking it up on the wall. This will become a useful reference point for getting the room back into order.

DIET

Be aware that certain foods will alter your child's stress and anxiety levels as well as create mood swings. Good foods to eat plenty of are: porridge, brown rice, wholegrain breads, fish, turkey, chicken, cottage cheese, pulses, nuts, fruit and vegetables in general. You can make crumble toppings for fruit pies by combining ground almonds with porridge oats and adding vegetable oil, cinnamon and maple syrup.

Other foods good for the mind are: brazil nuts because they are high in selenium and Vitamin E, fatty fish like salmon which contains plenty of Omega 3, good quality yoghurts with live bacteria, pumpkin and flax seeds and bananas that are not too ripe.

Latest studies show that depression and low mood can be linked to an inflammation in the brain and if you have a teenager that is struggling with these symptoms, I would arrange an appointment with a nutritionist or naturopath (in addition to your doctor) as they can arrange for a set of blood tests and offer advice.

It's also important to avoid toxins: caffeine and sugar are the two biggest culprits. Your child may not be drinking tea or coffee but there's plenty of caffeine in energy drinks. Beware the stimulating effects of sugar that create shaky, buzzy feelings similar to anxiety. Remember to think about the natural sugars found in fruit juices and smoothies – in an effort to be healthy our children are consuming far more fruit than previous generations. Supermarkets provide us with mangoes, pineapples and strawberries all year round and with Government advice telling us to eat five a day, children are filling up on more fruit than ever before.

SMELLS

The olfactory sense directly links to the amygdala, which is the emotional centre of our brain. Introduce calming smells into your home environment but avoid synthetically manufactured smells, the likes of which you'll find in cheap supermarket candles and sprays – they're made with toxic chemicals and are bad for the environment. Consider introducing more of these smells:

- Jasmine, bergamot and citrus smells will improve feelings of wellbeing.

- Peppermint, cinnamon and rosemary are good for the easily distracted.

- Lavender and chamomile aid restful sleep.

- Lavender and rosemary plants can be left around the house, especially in the bathroom as the steam will heighten the scent.

- Aim to use natural soaps in the bathroom – these are also better for the environment as they use less plastic. Your child will benefit from the smell as they wash their hands.

- During stressful exam times, I made a point of regularly putting an apple pie in the oven for my kids – not always home-made I have to confess, but the sight and smell of that pie as it came out of the oven somehow signified that all was well in the world and made everyone smile.

EXERCISE

When we feel anxious our bodies give us a massive injection of adrenaline and cortisol – those life-saving chemicals designed to help us flee danger or fight it. If your child spends many hours sitting slumped on the sofa playing computer games, you can be sure the excitement of these will trigger off those same stress chemicals. These chemicals turn into glucose energy and can give your child jittery, wobbly feelings that are very similar to feelings of anxiety. If this energy is not used for the purpose for which it was intended, i.e. to run away from danger, then the body will convert it into fat that then gets stored around the middle of the body, close to the liver. As we're seeing more evidence of a problem with obesity in childhood, I do wonder if this unused energy is to blame for some of this.

It's important to encourage your child to take plenty of exercise – not only will they burn off the unwanted stress chemicals but they'll also receive a nice injection of feelgood endorphins from the activity itself.

Studies show that kids who spend more time outdoors in nature are not only calmer and happier but also have improved sleep patterns and perform better at school.

In our society we're also surrounded by toxic electromagnetic frequencies (EMFs) and these also increase stress within the body. Encouraging your child to go outside daily and walk barefoot on grass, dirt or sand will enable them to absorb natural EMFs from the ground that will balance the electrical rhythms. Sitting on the ground, leaning up against trees and lying on grass are all ways of doing this.

PETS

The therapeutic benefits of owning a pet are becoming more widely recognised and many primary schools are now considering having a school dog. When we're anxious we spend a lot of time 'inside our heads' listening to unhelpful internal dialogue, and having a defenceless creature that needs thinking about and caring for will help to take the attention, awareness and focus away from ourselves. I'm not advocating everyone rushes to buy a puppy but if a pet would fit in with your family circumstances, have a conversation about the merits and what kind of animal would suit you best. The benefit of having a dog is of course, that more outdoor exercise will be taken, but do be aware that even the most enthusiastic of children will quickly break their promises of doing daily walks, so be prepared for a hefty amount of outdoor walking yourself. Coming home from a stressful day at school to snuggle up on the sofa with something soft, warm and furry has known health benefits for children, but if you're unsure whether a pet would be a good idea for your family, there are ways to 'try before you buy': you can offer to holiday-sit a friend's pet, visit pets at animal shelters and check out charities such as Pets as Therapy that will visit you at home with a dog.

LAUGH MORE

Laughing in response to day-to-day problems may not be an obvious choice for most of us, but it's one of the quickest ways to change your brain chemistry. Make watching funny movies together a regular habit – schedule it into the diary. Your child will benefit from the closeness that a regular family activity will foster. You can become a good role model by laughing at some of the difficult things that happen in your day e.g. forgetting front door keys and locking yourself out of the house. OK, it's not funny, but getting stressed and anxious about it will not help you to use your problem-solving skills and get back into the house any quicker. Make light of it and demonstrate to your child that not every problem in life needs to cause stress.

PRETEND PLAY

From the age of two years, you can start using dolls, teddy bears and story-telling to help explain difficult situations. You can take turns at playing 'Doctors' by giving a favourite teddy an injection or a dental examination. Older children might have a favourite TV character or super-hero and you could ask them to think about what they think this character would do if faced with the same challenging situation that they're in at the moment.

CREATE A VISION BOARD

Create a vision board in your child's bedroom and encourage them to pin pictures of things that make them feel happy on it. These could be puppies, kittens, footballers, ice-cream, best friends, family members, holiday snaps, theme park rides or favourite super-heroes. Ideally, I would position this on the wall opposite your child's bed so they can look at these pictures just before they fall asleep.

Alternatively, you can create a 'happy box' – somewhere to store trinkets and souvenirs of nice things, e.g. soft fluffy feathers, interesting shells, a small bell that rings, a piece of crystal, photos of favourite people and nice places.

Any time your child is feeling anxious or low, rather than trying to talk them out of it, you may find it's more effective for them to spend some quiet time looking through the contents of the box or thinking about what new pictures they could add to their vision board.

MUSIC

Having background music playing in the home can also help to create calm and soothing atmospheres. Neuroscientists at MindLab International carried out studies and came up with a list of therapeutic sound tracks. One track in particular – 'Weightless' by the group Marconi Union – resulted in a striking 65% reduction in participants' overall anxiety, and a 35% reduction in their usual physiological resting rates, as well as slowing down the listener's heart rate, reducing blood pressure and lowering levels of the stress hormone cortisol.

I can recommend listening to the radio station Chill – there are no news bulletins, no traffic updates, no weather reports – they don't even tell you the time. No-one speaks, it's just a constant stream of some of the loveliest music around. I would definitely recommend filling the home with something like this.

DIGITAL DETOX

I know many parents will be groaning at the thought of trying to police their child's screen use. Our daily lives include an ever-increasing number of screens and devices, and today's children can easily be glued to theirs for long periods of time.

According to a new study by San Diego State University professor of psychology Jean Twenge, there is a direct link between extended screen use and feelings of anxiety and depression in teenagers. Mental illnesses can be prevented with healthy parenting that sets limits on screen time.

So, what's the best way to set limits? It can be tricky to decide. Most parents didn't have such a wide range of technology when they were children, so find themselves ill-prepared to tackle such problems.

It's best to have a clear set of rules and boundaries in place – ones that you've carefully thought through and discussed as a family. Moaning at your children each time they whisk out their mobile phones at the dinner table is not setting boundaries and rules. It feels like it is – but it isn't.

Personally, I'm not in favour of strict time limits. It sounds like a sensible idea but I believe you could be storing up problems for the future. As technology advances, much more of your child's education is going to take place on a screen. All of a sudden, a half-term school project will eat into their time allocation and the whingeing and whining will start. You'll end up giving in and your child will learn that a good moan is exactly what they need to do in order to get the allocation of time extended.

You'll need to adopt the same rules that you're insisting your children follow and agree on a set of family guidelines – ones you've selected because they mean healthy, happy living. It may mean a family rule where no mobile phones are allowed at the dinner table or that they should not be carried around in trouser pockets all the time. If you make these rules, however, then you must abide by them too. It won't do to tell your child off for fiddling with their phone as you are scrolling through yours to check your emails.

It's helpful to create a family charging station – a dedicated place where everyone can leave their phone and tablet device when they're not in use. Get into a routine of doing this with your own devices and your children will automatically copy you. Kids are programmed to learn by copying the behaviours of those around them – do less nagging and more demonstrating of how to behave.

READ MORE: For more advice on how to create a family digital detox, see my other book, *Words that Work: How to Get Kids to Do Almost Anything.*

4

Let's talk

EXPRESSING EMOTIONS

Talking about our feelings helps us to feel close to the people around us and to feel better. Children will feel sad, nervous, angry, happy or embarrassed just as often as we do but without the vocabulary to express themselves the way we can.

It can be hard to teach kids about feelings because it's a fairly abstract concept – how do you describe how it feels to be sad, scared or excited?

It's quite common to hear young children complaining of a tummy ache or headache when they're feeling something different altogether. And that lack of vocabulary and self-awareness is often the cause behind many a child's moaning: one minute they're too hot and the next, they're too cold; one day they want milk poured on top of their cereal and the next day, they want it the other way round.

It seems there's no pleasing them and that's because the source of their discomfort does not match the complaint. When we experience a set of feelings that we can't quite figure out, we'll create a narrative to fit it – even if it's wide of the mark.

A child without the vocabulary skills might use actions instead, which can cause even more problems – temper tantrums, aggression or defiance – so it's good to teach children about their emotions from an early age. A child who can say *"I'm cross with you"* or *"That really upset me"* is less likely to lash out at another child.

A good way to start introducing the concept of emotions is to point out positive feelings to your child, e.g.: *"You look really happy that we're off to the park"* or *"You're excited that your friend is coming to play"*.

And then move on to point out negative emotions too – *"I can see that you're feeling cross those building bricks are so tricky to fit together"* or *"A long day at school can make us feel tired and crotchety"* or *"I can see you're sad that your friend can't come to play today"*.

Various experimental studies have found that if you speak or write down your emotional experiences, you can reduce feelings of distress – this is preferable to saying nothing at all.

Exercise: Words to Express Emotion

Take a look through these lists of words and practise incorporating more of them into your everyday language when chatting to your child.

Happy	Strong	Good	Afraid	Hurt	Sad
great	eager	calm	fearful	upset	tearful
lucky	keen	peaceful	terrified	pained	sorrowful
fortunate	sure	comfortable	anxious	dejected	pained
delighted	certain	pleased	alarmed	rejected	grief
jolly	inspired	clever	panic	injured	anguish
sparkling	determined	content	nervous	offended	desolate
overjoyed	excited	quiet	scared	aching	desperate
thankful	enthusiastic	certain	worried	heartbroken	pessimistic
ecstatic	bold	relaxed	frightened	appalled	unhappy
satisfied	brave	bright	timid	humiliated	lonely
pleased	optimistic	commendable	shaky	wronged	down in the dumps
glad	confident	splendid	restless	alienated	out of sorts
cheerful	hearty	admirable	doubtful	distressed	blue
thrilled	capable	agreeable	threatened	disturbed	dejected
tickled pink	robust	exceptional			despondent
sunny	solid	marvellous			troubled
	able				

WORDS THAT WORK

In Chapter 2, I explained how we are constantly creating images inside our minds, even if we're not completely aware of them. Our bodies respond to those images and will take them as a prompt on what to do next.

The key to helping your child overcome anxiety is to ensure that they have the right images to focus upon and these will be determined to an extent by the words and language that you use around them. It's important to become more aware of the language that you use, for your words may stay with your child for the rest of their lives.

How many of us can remember being told that we were *'not sporty'* or *'not good at maths'*? That we were *'shy'* or the *'quiet one'*? Or perhaps the one who was *'always getting into trouble'* or *'noisy'*. These words become part of our self-image and when that self-image is a negative one, it's very difficult to break out of that thinking pattern and become or do something different. How different would your life have been if you had heard different words being spoken by the adults around you?

Become aware too, of the times when your child might have had the opportunity to overhear you speaking about their fear or phobia to another family member or friend. Even very young children will be listening to your words, keenly absorbing every one of them. If you do want to discuss your child's fears with someone, make sure it's out of earshot.

When a child is struggling with an anxiety issue it's even more important to ensure that your vocabulary is appropriate for guiding them into a calmer, happier state.

In this section, I'll show you how changing just a few of your words can create a change in your child's attitude and behaviour:

1. SAY WHAT YOU *DO* WANT, RATHER THAN WHAT YOU *DON'T*

One of the quickest and simplest ways to get more helpful thoughts and images into your child's mind is to encourage them to be thinking about what they **do want**, rather than what they don't. Remember how your mind created images for you in response to the questions I asked you in the exercise (p. 20)? As I pointed out, we're naturally drawn to the images inside our mind and act in accordance with them almost as if we're on auto-pilot so it's important to ensure the best possible images are inside your child's mind.

Exercise

Ask your child to imagine they're sitting in a restaurant and the menu offers them a choice of:

- margherita pizza
- spaghetti bolognese
- burger and fries
- chicken salad

Now ask them to choose one of those meals. Let's say they decide they'd like to eat the pizza. When the waiter comes up to take their order, what would happen if your child said: *"I don't want the burger and fries and I don't want the chicken"*?

Ask your child to think about how the waiter would respond to that.

It wouldn't be very positive, would it, because they won't know what your child does want to eat and so won't be able to fetch it. In order to have the pizza, you have to tell the waiter exactly what you *do* want to eat – not what you *don't*. And life is a bit like that too – we need to be specific when it comes to ordering off the 'menu of life'.

Negative words create obstacles in the mind and thereby obstacles in real life, making it harder for us to move forward. You may have heard of 'the power of positive thinking' and perhaps, the 'Law of Attraction'. Sometimes these are referred to in quite simplistic terms – just think about what you want and it will fall into your lap. I'm not surprised some people are sceptical about whether this truly works.

But what's often not fully explained is that the reason it's important to think positively, is because our mind converts our thoughts into those mental images and we will find ourselves magnetically drawn to behaving in just that way.

Take a look at these sentences:

I'm scared I might forget my lines in the school play.
will not help as much as:
I'm going to remember all my lines for the school play tomorrow speaking loudly and clearly.

I hope I don't come last in the running race.
will not work as well as:
I'm going to run faster than I ever have before in tomorrow's race.

I'm too scared to go into the park in case that nasty dog is there.
will not put you in a resourceful state so it's better to say:
I want to feel calm and relaxed when I go into the park tomorrow.

I'm worried I might not have anyone to talk to at the party.
is not as helpful as:
I'm curious about who I'll meet at the party tomorrow.

I'm worried I might forget all the answers for the test tomorrow.
won't work as well as:
I want to remember all the correct answers in tomorrow's spelling test.

When you see yourself failing, coming last or losing out, your chances of succeeding are drastically diminished.

Remind your child that just like ordering food off that menu, ordering exactly what you would like will work so much better. Even if they're not entirely convinced that changing those few words will help, encourage them to re-phrase their words into the positive on a regular basis. This is also called behaving 'as if' – even though you know you're not quite there yet, acting 'as if' you already are and can indeed do it, changes the brain chemistry sufficiently to create the all-important difference between success and failure.

Exercise

Let's test this out. In the exercise (p. 20), I asked you to think about a few things and notice the images that popped into your mind, such as:

- what you had eaten for breakfast
- the capital of France
- your dream holiday destination

Now I'm going to ask you to do this:

- Pause for a moment and don't think of a piece of chocolate cake.

Hmmm . . . I wonder how many of you did exactly what I asked you not to? Even though I asked you *not* to think of a piece of cake, most of you will have seen one – it may have been a slice, a whole round cake or a square of brownie. You may even have seen a cherry on the top or some ice-cream with it!

There are no pictures for the words 'don't, no, not, never' and so on, so as soon as you think of what you don't want, you will inevitably see it. And what you see is what you get. If you've ever said *"don't touch the vase"* to a child and wondered why they did exactly that, now you'll understand why. It's better to say *"let's leave the vase alone"*.

And if your child can't seem to remember to take the correct books to school with them each morning, ask yourself whether you regularly use the phrase *"don't forget . . ."*

So phrases such as *"don't worry"* are really not helpful because all your child will see is an image of themselves worrying! A child recently told me that in his school a teacher had written *"Remember, don't panic"* on the back of the exam papers. She thought she was being helpful, but it was the first thing the children saw before turning over their papers to begin the exam. What an image to have in your mind just at this critical moment. *"Remember to breathe and remain calm"* would have been so much better. I like the word *'remain'* too, because there's an automatic suggestion that your child was feeling calm in the first place.

2. THINK ABOUT IT

There can be times when it's tricky to get your child to focus only on the positive, so one way to help with this is to front-load your sentences with the phrase *"Think about it"*. This acts as a command to encourage your child's mind to do just that:

- *Think about it. How good will it feel once the exam is over?*

- *Think about it. Won't it be good to come out of the dentist knowing our teeth are healthy and clean?*

- *Think about it. Isn't it better to look at this differently?*

3. CAN-DO PHRASES

The word *'can't'* can be used far too often in conversations, shutting out the possibility of achievement. To get out of this habit, highlight that things can and do change. Indeed, your child is changing all the time, which means not being able to do something is merely transient:

- When your child says: *"I can't do maths!"*

  Turn it around into: *"Ah, you just haven't yet found a way to . . ."* Switch the focus to talk about what your child *can* do rather than what they *can't*:

> *"You can add, subtract, multiply and divide. . . . You just haven't yet found a way to do fractions. Don't forget, things change. We all change all the time – and learning how to do fractions is just one more of those things that will gradually change."*

This will start to alter your child's attitude.

It may help to remind your child of struggles that they've had in the past that they successfully overcame:

- *"You know, once upon a time, you couldn't swim backstroke – do you remember? You splashed and struggled – and to be honest, even I was starting to wonder if you'd ever get the hang of it.* (Add a smile and a wink to show you are teasing.)

- *And then, look what happened. All of a sudden, one day, something just clicked and now . . . well, now . . . you're one of the best backstroke swimmers in the class. Just because you can't do something right now, doesn't mean you never will – it just means you haven't found a way to do it yet."*

You can also point out to your child that they are changing all the time. In sessions, I find it useful to point out that *"once upon a time you couldn't walk and you couldn't talk – you couldn't read and you couldn't write your name, but now you can do those things so very easily. . . . Things change and you change and learning how to . . . (insert desired behaviour) . . . is just one more those things you can easily do."*

Sometimes I even point out that they're growing and changing all the time – their hair needs trimming from time to time; their feet grow larger and require new shoes; they outgrow their trousers and need the next size up. Childhood is a fluid, dynamic state – nothing stays the same for very long and tapping into this changing energy is the ideal time to change those thought processes and create new and different outcomes.

4. NEVER 'TRY' ANYTHING

Follow this exercise to see how one tiny little word can so easily create a negative picture and hold you back. Why not test it out on a friend or colleague? Ask them to close their eyes and follow your instructions and have them do the same to you.

Exercise

1. Close your eyes and see in your imagination a door.

2. Notice the colour of the door and say the colour out loud.

3. Open the door.

4. When you have opened the door, open your eyes.

PAUSE

5. Close your eyes again and see in your imagination another door.

6. Notice the colour of the door and say the colour out loud.

7. Now this time, try to open the door.

PAUSE

8. Open your eyes and come back into the room.

- What difference did you find between the first door and the second door?

- Were the doors the same colour, or different?

- Did they have handles, locks or bolts?

- Were the handles on the same side?

- Did the doors open slowly or quickly?

As you'll discover, most people find it's a struggle to open the door the second time around and yet the words are pretty much the same. Some of you will have noticed that in the second part of the exercise, I inserted the word 'try' – and just look at the results!

When the word 'try' is used, it makes it so much harder for us to achieve what we want. We'll find it difficult, or we'll not be able to do it at all, as the suggestion is that there will be a struggle and then it becomes just that.

This is an interesting exercise and will probably make you think back to your own childhood. How many times did someone say to you: *"As long as you try, that's all that matters"*, or *"Try your best"* or *"Just try and have a go"*?

Likewise encouraging your child to *'try their hardest'* when setting off to face a challenge in the morning is not the best thing to say, for twice in that phrase you'll have suggested it's going to be difficult.

Using the word 'try' can also suggest that this is something to be feared – for example, in the case of a fussy-eater: *"just try one mouthful"* is supposed to be helpful but actually suggests that there's something wrong with the food as surely, you'd be encouraging them to eat more than one mouthful if it were delicious?

5. BECOME

A very useful word is 'become'. It's another way of suggesting progression, a change of direction and that things are moving forward:

- *And as you become more and more relaxed about this each and every day . . .*

- *As each week passes, you're becoming a much better swimmer . . .*

More words that suggest things are changing and moving forward are:

- *And as you start noticing yourself becoming more and more successful with each and every attempt to . . .*

- *As you start to change the way you organise your revision, you'll quickly see the difference it makes.*

- *I can see by looking at that relaxed smile on your face that a transformation is taking place.*

- *You'll be surprised by how quickly you'll be able to stop making those mistakes and start getting more of the answers right.*

- *That's great – you've already come up with three new ways of getting that done. I expect you've thought of a few more too.*

6. PUTTING IT IN THE PAST

Another way of giving positive suggestions to your child that they can and will get over their fears is to give the illusion that they're already halfway there. This may be a little bit of a 'white lie' but sometimes just having a confident parent to support and show the way forward is all a child needs to start making changes:

- *You used to be (so scared of spiders) but now you're finding it much easier to manage. I wonder if you've noticed?*

- *There was a time when you really struggled to fall asleep in the evenings (because you were scared of the dark) but I noticed the other night that you managed to do this more easily.*

- *I wonder when you'll start becoming aware that you feel different?*

- *Isn't it nice to know that these happy feelings are becoming more a part of your everyday life?*

- *And now that you're on the way, how good are things going to be once you've solved this problem?*

7. EMPATHISE

Certain phrases imply that you can see into your child's mind and understand what they're going through. This enables you to show empathy, despite the fact that they may not have shared or verbalised their feelings with you yet, if indeed they ever will.

Use phrases such as:

- *I can see that . . .*

- *I sense that . . .*

- *I understand that . . .*

- *I wonder what extra help you'd need right now and how you'd start to use it?*

- *This isn't working well is it? What shall we do to fix it?*

- *What do you think you need right now?*

8. WHAT TO SAY IN MOMENTS OF PANIC

It can be hard to come up with the right words when your child is in a state of panic, because understandably, seeing them in a state of panic can trigger off those same feelings in ourselves. Learning a few key phrases for moments when your child has been stung by a wasp, frightened by a dog, has witnessed a distressing event or feels as if they're having an asthma attack will help you manage situations more effectively:

- *I'm going to help you through this.*

- *The worst is over and everything will start to get better from now on.*

- *It feels like something is wrong, but these feelings are harmless – you are absolutely fine.*

- *You're not in danger – you're safe right now. Your brain is sending the wrong signal – you'll be fine.*

- *You got scared about what these feelings meant but the anxiety will pass in a couple of moments.*

- *Breathe with me, let's slow it down.*

- *I can see it's hard for you to get comfortable but you can slowly allow yourself to begin feeling calmer even if the anxiety is there.*

- *As you begin to slow your breathing down, you'll notice how much easier things are starting to feel.*

- *Walk with me over here so I can help you start to feel better and as you do, keep holding my hand.*

- *Just because you're scared doesn't mean you are in danger.*

- *Anxious feelings always go away – have you ever had an anxious feeling that didn't?*

READ MORE: You'll find more examples of how to use the language of persuasion in my book, *Words that Work: How to Get Kids to Do Almost Anything*.

MEETING AS A FAMILY

Now that you have a better idea of what to say to a child who's suffering from anxiety, the next step will be to discuss the problem so that together you can begin to come up with solutions and a plan for moving forward.

I know that for some of you, this won't be an issue as you're already talking about it, perhaps on a daily basis. But many of you will be avoiding any talk about the problem for fear of making it worse or adding to the embarrassment. Even if it feels challenging, most people find that once things are out in the open, everyone breathes a sigh of relief.

If the idea of having a face-to-face conversation feels tricky, think about having it when you're driving along in the car or walking side by side. For older children and teenagers, you could even consider a late evening stroll outside by torch light, whilst star-gazing or hunting for nocturnal wildlife. Fostering feelings of closeness will help you discuss tricky problems more easily.

I really recommend having regular family group conversations as these will help to inoculate your children from the difficulties and challenges they encounter in daily life. Good family communication is key to raising resilient kids.

You can call your regular chats whatever you feel will suit your family: a meetup; circle time; round table; think-in; forum; get-together; powwow; session; weekly talk. It doesn't matter what you call it, but it is important that families put time in the diary for being together as a group. As wonderful as today's technological advances are, with the advent of computers, smartphones and online streaming networks, we all know that when every person in the house has their own device, it's easy to lose sight of each other despite living under the same roof.

WHAT TO TALK ABOUT

It's good to start your group meetings with some good news – do you have any positive things to talk about? Discussing future plans such as holidays or whether to have a barbeque at the weekend is a nice, neutral way of starting a conversation. You can then go around the group and ask if anyone has any good or funny news they'd like to share. It will set the tone for the meeting and your children will see it as an enjoyable practice.

Your family get-together will then ideally become a safe, comfortable place for all the family members to discuss their worries and problems too.

A PROBLEM SHARED IS A PROBLEM HALVED

I've worked with many children who have insisted on keeping their fear, phobia or anxiety a secret from siblings and other family members. In essence they then have two problems – the issue itself and secondly, worries about being teased or made fun of for having the problem in the first place.

We all know that making light of a problem and having a laugh about it can help enormously in allowing us to get a sense of proportion and balance. But no child should ever be made to feel stupid for their fears and worries – it's part of having a healthy human mind. It would be strange and unusual to never experience feelings of fear – and dangerous too, for these can save our lives.

Opening up and confessing to a problem is a huge step as we automatically make ourselves vulnerable to the group which goes against our natural survival instincts, so any child who does this should be applauded. But once it's out in the open, you can then brainstorm as a family and go round the group, coming up with possible solutions to the problem. These can be written down – aim to get at least ten items on the list – and then the child with the problem can discard the suggestions that don't appeal and think about ways to utilise and implement the solution that does.

Coming up with a long list of solutions will teach your child that it's OK to be creative and think outside the box. There's nothing wrong with coming up with an idea that on reflection, turns out not to be a good idea after all. There's no shame, no blame – only praise for making the list of possible solutions even longer. And the most outlandish, wacky idea can get a great big laugh – in fact, I'd recommend that all adults come up with a silly idea that gets thrown out, simply to show that it's not the end of the world to get it wrong and get laughed at.

And if one child in the family decides they are going to work on getting over their fear of dogs for example, or manage anxiety caused by school exams, then that would be an ideal time for other members of the group to also share a worry or two to show this is a normal part of everyday life. But I recommend you keep the matter pretty light – now is not the time to confess that you're worried you might lose your job or fail to pay the mortgage! Spider phobia anyone?

TIPS TO GET KIDS TALKING

It's all good and well planning a get-together meeting for the family, but what happens if your kids just aren't 'talkers'? Or what if one of them dominates the conversation and you find the others are happy to stay quiet?

If you're starting your get-togethers with young children, it's very likely that you won't have too many problems in getting them to contribute. But if you're introducing these meetings for the first time to older children or teenagers, there may be an element of distrust on their part and a reluctance to participate. Follow these tips:

- **Remember to use open questions:** Start sentences with words like *What, Why, Where, How* rather than *Did you . . .*

- **Ask for more details:** *And what was the best bit about that . . . / Then what happened? / I'm intrigued . . . what happened next? / So, tell me more . . .*

- **Make observations:** *You looked like you really enjoyed that / I can see that you put extra effort in doing that well . . . / That's interesting . . .*

- **Give 100% attention:** We get cross with our kids if we're talking to them and they don't seem to be listening. It's a horrible feeling and we end up wondering if there's any point in continuing. Your child will feel exactly the same. So, if they're talking to you, you must give them your full attention and look at them. That means no checking your phone, writing things in a notepad, picking your fingernails, feeding the cat, emptying the washing machine, etc. Or one day, you'll find that they will simply give up and stop talking to you altogether.

- **You don't have to solve every problem:** Have you ever tried to tell a friend about a problem you're experiencing, only to have them interrupt every few sentences by offering a solution? Annoying isn't it? And often the advice they give is inappropriate and if only they would listen to the end of the story, they'd know and understand that! It's the same for your child. Sometimes they just need to get something off their chest to feel better. So if you're hearing that they were pushed over at school, a simple *"Oh, that's not nice – were you hurt anywhere?"* may be enough. As much as you may want to rush into school to tell the other child off and report it to the teachers, your child isn't asking you to do that – they just want a sympathetic ear and probably a hug.

HOW OFTEN SHOULD YOU HAVE YOUR REGULAR MEETINGS?

Little and often is good for young children. You can keep the meetings to a short 15 or 20 minutes and have them once or even twice a week. Older children and teenagers might start feeling a little 'under the spotlight' if they're too frequent so once every two weeks is probably better. If you start having them as little as once a month, I suspect you'll lose the feeling of continuity and a sense of "oh, what am I going to get told off about now" will start to creep in.

WHERE TO HAVE THE MEETING

Having your regular family chats around the table at mealtimes may seem convenient but I do not recommend this. It's not good for children to feel anxious as they eat as this in itself could create yet more problems. Eating as a family should be a relaxed, enjoyable time.

Your family meeting doesn't even have to take place formally around a table, although sometimes it can be useful to have a table to sit round to harness attention and make it easier to focus. You may also want to write things down on paper or notebook on your laptop or tablet.

But it could also be:

- Sitting in a circle on a rug on the living room floor.

- On a blanket in the garden.

- As part of a picnic in the park.

- On a bed surrounded by comfy cushions.

- Parked up in the car – or even in a traffic jam.

In fact, I would recommend that you pick a different or more unusual location now and again, especially if you find your meetings not going as well as you'd like them to. Don't stick to the same seating plan every time – it's good to shuffle places and you might find your children are more creative and relaxed in a different seat.

Always take time after the meeting to reflect: how well did things go? What worked well and what didn't? What could you do better next time – and how? These are good habits to develop and will serve your family well for many years to come.

5

Tools to help

MEASUREMENT SCALES

When helping people overcome problems with anxiety I commonly ask them to rate the intensity of their feelings on a scale of one to ten. It can be useful to do this at the start of a session when they arrive, so that I can then compare it to how they feel after we've worked through their issues. It can give an indication that things are moving in the right direction and creates valuable proof and evidence for the person that they can quickly help themselves to feel better using the techniques I teach them.

Children will find it much harder to rate their anxiety using a number scale and so I like to use visual cues – see Figure 1 overleaf – a measurement scale showing a line of faces ranging from happy to really worried.

In the next few sections, I'm going to be showing you a range of exercises and techniques that you can use with your child to help alleviate their feelings of anxiety. A good starting point will be to take a reading on the measurement scale by asking them to point to the face that most represents the way they feel right now. Then you can move on, saying *"Let's follow this exercise and see how we feel then"*. When you've finished the activity, take another reading by asking your child to rate the intensity of their feelings on the scale once more. Their score rating will either have moved in a positive direction, in which case everyone will be feeling happy, or it won't, in which case you'll need to repeat the activity or think about a different approach. Either way, it's useful to have some feedback.

Figure 1 MEASUREMENT SCALE

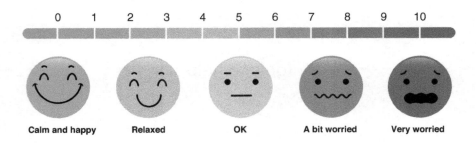

GETTING A GOAL IN PLACE

Some types of anxiety may take a longer, more consistent approach (e.g. overcoming separation anxiety or school refusal) and putting a targeted action plan in place will help you to do this.

Think about it - if you do not know what your final destination is, how will you know that you've got there? If your child's particular problem is a one-off attack of nerves in response to an interview or exams, then you won't necessarily need to do this and some straightforward relaxation techniques and visualisation exercises might be all you need.

The more specific and clear your child can be about how they'd like to feel, the greater the chances of success. There can be times when it may not be so easy to put this into words – some children can feel that there isn't really anything that they want, all they know is what they don't want - and that is to stop the unwanted feelings of anxiety and misery.

Together you can write out a clearly defined goal answering these questions:

1. *Is the end goal stated in positive terms?*

   - *"I want to go to school feeling happy and relaxed"* rather than *"I don't want to be nervous about going to school"*.

- *"I want to feel relaxed at night-time and sleep well"* rather than *"I don't want to keep being scared of the dark"*.

- *"I want to feel calm in the run-up to the exams and remember all the information"* rather than *"I want to stop worrying about my exams"*.

2. **Can you achieve this goal by yourself or will you need help from others around you?**
Identify all the resources and people that your child might need to assist them in achieving the positive outcome. Perhaps you could include a couple of people you know who had a similar problem in the past and ask them how they solved it.

3. **Is the context clearly defined? How will it be achieved – when, where, how, who?**
Having established the goal, be very specific about what it is your child is aiming for. If it's being able to take part in the school play, write down all the steps that need to be taken before attending the audition.
A larger outcome such as passing an entrance exam to a new school or university may have to be broken into smaller chunks. Will they need to do more studying, invest in extra tuition or acquire new skills such as interview techniques for example?

4. **Remember to include all the senses when writing out the goal.**
Having defined the outcome in specific terms, establish some sensory-based evidence. How will your child know when they have reached their goal? They may 'know' they want to be able to stand on stage and sing confidently but what will that look like exactly? What will they see, hear and feel when they finally achieve their ambition?

REWARD SYSTEMS

There's conflicting advice about whether offering rewards as an additional incentive to help children overcome their anxieties is appropriate. On the face of it, some sort of recognition in the form of a coveted item does sound like a good idea – surely if your child is going to be expected to push themselves to overcome a problem, then a soothing carrot may well make all the difference to their level of motivation.

Rewarding and praising children – rather than punishing and disciplining – has grown in popularity to such a degree that few of us stop to question whether it's actually a good idea. Most people do it simply because it just 'feels' like good parenting.

However, I would encourage you to think again. Studies now show that when children expect or anticipate rewards, they can actually end up achieving less. Not only do they start to become very reliant on outside validation rather than developing a good sense of how they're feeling on the inside, but offering a new pair of trainers, say, to combat a school refusal problem takes the focus and awareness off the main goal. It's a mental distraction for your child as they'll have images of trainers in their mind rather than seeing themselves returning to school feeling calm and confident. It may work in the short-term but what's going to happen when the novelty of the new trainers has worn off – and perhaps some feelings of anxiety start to return? Your child will be looking round for the next 'reward' to compensate for not feeling great and as they become adults, we know that compensatory rewards can easily turn to less healthy options.

Of course, there has to be something positive to be gained out of any kind of challenge, otherwise there would be no point in doing it. But encourage your child to keep the end goal in their mind as their 'reward', for this will increase their chances of getting there.

This does not mean you'll never be giving your child a 'treat' again, but this can be given for different reasons. For example, in the case of school refusal it would work something like this:

"Once you're settled back at school, we both know you'll enjoy seeing your friends again on a daily basis and spending more time with them. Callum has said he's looking forward to having you sitting next to him again. (REWARD) At the end of term, we could have a trip to the cinema and go out for something to eat with him, couldn't we? (TREAT)"

KEEPING A DIARY OR JOURNAL

Sometimes the use of a daily star chart is recommended for getting over a problem, e.g. sleeping through the night or a separation anxiety issue, but I would exercise caution. Star charts are similar to reward systems and if things don't go well one day your child has the double disappointment of not being successful and then also missing out on a star. On the other hand, keeping a 'Success Journal' or 'Diary' to track progress is a good idea – for studies have shown that what gets measured automatically improves. This is ideal for those situations that can take a bit longer to solve – it's easy to forget any progress that's been made so being able to look back will help your child. And if they do slip backwards for some reason, having the ability to see that they have already made some progress will help keep them motivated to put effort into it.

Keeping a full diary will also give you the opportunity to look back and ask the question: *"What happened in the previous 24 hours?"* if your child happens to have had a bad day. Take some time to think about whether it was a busy, stressful school day or a lazy day in the holidays with too much screen time. Did they get plenty of sleep or did they have a late night because of too much school work? Did they go to a friend's birthday party and overload on sugar? All this is valuable information.

DOWNLOAD: You can download a free 30-day Success Journal from my website.

SECTION THREE

FIRST AID TECHNIQUES AND STRATEGIES

In this section, I'm going to be giving you details of the kinds of methods that I regularly use with children in my Harley Street clinic. This can act as a resource for you to refer to as and when you need a solution to a particular problem.

You might find it more convenient to skim through these techniques to begin with as you'll gain a better understanding of how to use them when you read through Section 4, which is where I give details on how I helped a number of children overcome a variety of different problems, using these methods. You'll then be able to come back to this section to study the techniques in more detail.

6

Let's relax

Relaxation can come in many forms and taking some time to stretch and tense muscles before relaxing them can a very effective way of working stress out of the body. For younger children, learning to relax can be made fun. I recommend fitting these exercises into your weekly routine.

Stretch and Tense Relaxation Exercise

1. March straight and upright around the room.
2. Run on the spot.
3. Pretend your arms are the branches of a tree by waving them above your head.
4. Screw up your face to look like a scary monster.
5. Stretch up to the sky and be as tall as possible.
6. Roll up tightly to become as small as possible.
7. Tightly squeeze your hands into a fist – and then release them again. Repeat.

Now, let's calm down and relax:

1. Pretend to be a big, heavy animal lumbering around the room very slowly.
2. Pretend you're a mouse, moving as quietly and as slowly as possible.
3. Become a 'sleeping lion' by lying on the floor and keeping as still and quiet as possible for a couple of minutes.

Progressive Relaxation Exercise

This passive, progressive relaxation exercise gradually works through each part of the body, bringing it slowly down to a complete stop. Use the step-by-step instructions below to gently guide your child into a nice calm, relaxed state. Speak slowly and quietly as you do this; if you prefer you can also have some relaxing music playing in the background. This is an ideal exercise for bedtime.

Have your child settle comfortably on a bed, sofa or on the floor with a cushion under their head – somewhere they can feel relaxed and comfortable.

Explain that you'll be doing an exercise to help their body relax and feel ten times more comfortable than it does right now. You may want to introduce ideas such as becoming as 'limp as a rag doll', 'wobbly like jelly' or similar.

1. Ask your child to close their eyes and become aware of their breathing. Tell them they may even be able to hear their breathing in their ears as it starts to slow down. Give them a minute to do this.

2. It's time to let the head relax. Ask them to scrunch up the eyes tightly for 3 seconds and then release and open again. Repeat and then let the eyes gently close.

3. Time to think about the jaw muscles now. Ask your child do a big, wide smile, clenching their teeth and to hold this for 3 seconds again. And then let the jaw completely relax by becoming slack and limp – perhaps their mouth will want to remain slightly open at this point.

4. Moving down the body to the shoulders – ask them to pull these up to their ears and hold for 3 seconds. Then release and let go.

5. Now it's the turn of the arms – bend each elbow so the wrist nearly touches the shoulder (one at a time), hold for 3 seconds and then relax and let the arms gently flop down.

6. Moving down to the hands – clench each hand into a fist one at a time and again hold for a few seconds and then release. Encourage your child to notice how each part of their body is starting to relax now and perhaps even starting to feel heavy.

7. Next, move down through the body – point out that their tummy will start to feel more relaxed as their breathing continues to move through this area.

8. And now the back begins to feel as if it is sinking deeper and deeper into the bed or sofa. Feeling good now . . . feeling relaxed.

9. The calming, relaxing flow of energy begins to travel down to the legs – perhaps your child will want to gently shake these out before allowing them to rest and come to a complete stop.

10. Now you can give suggestions that their feet will want to point to the bottom of the bed or sofa and then flop open and relax along with the rest of their body.

11. Tell your child that now the lovely, calming, relaxing feeling has come all the way through their body – from the top of their head all the way down to the tips of their toes - they'll be feeling good, feeling calm, feeling relaxed.

12. What colour would they like to give this feeling of relaxation? Can they imagine this special colour travelling through their body like a magical wave of lovely energy?

Encourage your child to stay in this position for at least 5 minutes if possible. Regular practice will help them to relax more quickly and they'll find it easier to stay like this for longer.

The final suggestion given should be that "when they are ready, they'll be able to easily open their eyes and come back into the room once more". Some children may fall asleep during this exercise and that's OK too. If you find this happens to your child, this may be a useful exercise to do at bedtime.

BREATHING TECHNIQUES

Anxiety can lead to a shortness of breath. This leads to a pale complexion, sweaty hands and face, tightness in the chest and even giddiness or fainting. *"Take a nice deep breath"* is a traditional response and is a phrase we're all familiar with, but taking a deep inward breath is precisely what an anxious person doesn't need to do. Anxious feelings can be caused by having too much air trapped in the lungs, which gives that sensation of not being able to breathe properly.

All the symptoms I've just described are very similar to the symptoms of asthma so it's not uncommon to hear adults who were diagnosed with asthma as children say they realise now that they were in fact experiencing an anxiety or panic attack.

Either way, the initial response to either an asthma or anxiety attack is much the same. It's very useful, if not important, to teach your child some basic breathing control through practice exercises before an emergency situation strikes. I recommend playing breathing 'games' on a regular basis, for you never know when they'll come in handy and the child that is used to controlling their breathing will fare much better.

All of us feel so much better after doing some deep breathing as this is one way our bodies can expel stress chemicals that accumulate over time. It's the reason why we also feel better after a good old cry – we eliminate stress toxins in our tears too.

BLOW IT OUT

Toys can help children practice blowing out and controlling their breathing and this is a useful way to introduce the concept to them. Some examples of these are:

- a hand-held windmill toy with sails;

- a container of bubble mixture to blow through a wand;

- blowing balloons;

- blowing bubbles in a drink through a straw;

- blow football;

- or placing a feather on the table and blowing it across to the other side.

You can also ask your child to scrunch up their hand and simply imagine that they're blowing up a balloon or paper bag – long, slow breathing out is what's required.

Counting Breaths Exercise

1. Ask your child to make themselves comfortable, take a deep breath in and then blow out for as long as they possibly can. If it helps, they can put their hand around their mouth creating something imaginary to blow into, such as a balloon or paper bag.

2. As they start blowing out, you can begin to slowly count out loud – or they can count silently to themselves: 1 . . . 2 . . . 3 . . . 4 . . . 5 . . . etc.

3. Take this slowly and steadily, as racing along with your counting will put them off.

4. Ask them to keep their attention on the breathing and not to allow other thoughts to creep into their minds.

5. When your child runs out of puff, record the number that they reached. How many seconds were they able to stretch that breath out for?

6. Now ask them to repeat the process. Breathe in deeply and blow a long slow breath out again. And you can start to count again.

7. Second time around, the aim is to beat the score achieved with the previous blow.

8. When they've run out of puff, you can record the score again. You can make a comment such as: *That was a bit longer wasn't it? First time around you scored 8 and now you've been able to blow out till you reached the number 10.*

9. Repeat this process again – *Let's see what number we get to third time around, shall we?*

To make it easier to get into the higher figures, there are a couple of things that you can do to help:

1. When they hear you say a number, ask them to *see* it at the same time say: *I wonder what colour and size your numbers will be.*

2. Ask your child to look out of a window – find an object in the distance and ask them to imagine blowing out a long, slow breath until they feel their breath has reached it.

MINDFULNESS MADE EASY

We often hear that 'Living in the moment' or 'Mindfulness' can reduce stress and greatly enhance the quality of our lives – it's an excellent way of reducing your child's feelings of anxiety. Children who have mental health issues can benefit from learning mindfulness practices, but it's not just for those who are having a difficult time but for all children. I'm pleased to see that mindfulness practice is becoming a part of the school day for many children.

Children are rarely still and quiet nowadays thanks to continuous stimulation from out-of-school activities and hand-held electronic devices that offer round-the-clock entertainment, never mind their supply of adrenaline pumping computer games. It's not surprising that it's becoming harder for them to keep a lid on their emotions and think before they act. Achieving a state of complete silence, peace and calm is way out of reach for most children.

Based on Buddhist philosophy, 'mindfulness' is a deliberate way of being and research shows that people who practise the art of observation – deliberately making a point of noticing all the tiny details of each moment – report decreased stress levels and a greater sense of happiness. The benefits are certainly worth having and with just a little bit of practice you too can begin to live your life mindfully and encourage your child to do the same.

It's not uncommon for our minds to flip between the past (to things that happened even 5 minutes ago) and the future (to things that you're planning). In doing so, it's possible to completely 'miss the moment' in life and stumble through it without ever getting to appreciate the good parts.

How many of us miss out on the joy of Christmas because we're stressing about the credit card bill we'll be receiving in January?

And this doesn't just happen to adults – have you ever taken your child to a friend's birthday party and watched them miss out on the fun and games because they were fussing and obsessing about whether their coat would be safe in the cloakroom, what they'd be given to eat later and whether they'd be collected on time when the party finishes?

Although most of the studies into mindfulness are based on adults, early research suggests that children may benefit in similar ways to:

- feel calmer and more fulfilled

- get on better with others

- concentrate better and produce improved academic results

- manage their stress and anxiety

- manage performance more effectively in areas such as sport, music and drama.

But despite the fact that mindfulness has become so popular and seemingly the cure to all ills, it's not always that easy to follow. When you're feeling stressed and anxious with a mind that's buzzing with thoughts, just being told to sit still and empty your mind can make you ten times madder, can't it?

So, there are a few mindfulness exercises that I really recommend – these can be incorporated into your everyday lives and will produce those same positive benefits without being specifically classed as mindfulness practice.

Mindfulness in Action

Take your child for a walk outside and as you're walking, begin to describe everything that you see, thus creating a running commentary:

- *The leaves on that tree are very green.*
- *There's a brown dog running quickly on the other side of the street.*
- *That lorry has big black wheels and a noisy engine.*
- *The sun is shining brightly today and there are clouds in the sky.*

- *There's a warm breeze on my face, can you feel it too?*
- *I can hear the sound of the gravel crunching as we walk across the path.*

You can also use this technique on simple activities that you do around the house, such as washing hands:

- *I can see you turning on the hot tap and now adding some cold water too.*
- *The soap is very green – I'm wondering, is it cold to the touch?*
- *You're squirting the soap on your left hand and rubbing it against the right hand now.*
- *It looks slippery and I can see you're making lots of bubbles.*
- *I can hear the water gurgling down the plughole – that's a funny sound isn't it?*
- *Does the soap have a pleasant smell to it? I think I can smell apples.*
- *You're switching the hot tap off with your left hand and now the cold tap too.*
- *Drying your hands now with the blue striped towel. Feeling soft to the touch.*

Notice how I've attempted to incorporate all the senses. Remember to think about what your child can see, hear, feel, smell and even taste. This is a great exercise to do whilst eating too. Think of not only the taste of the food but also the look of it; the bright colours; the texture; does it crunch as you eat it; and of course, the smell.

To begin with this may feel rather strange, but supplying this running commentary will encourage your child to 'stay in the moment', calm down their thoughts and snap them out of needless worrying and ruminating. This is especially good to incorporate into the bedtime routine – perhaps in the bath – when worries about the next school day may begin to surface.

The Mindfulness Jar

Create a 'mindfulness jar' by asking your child to fill an empty jar (the larger the better) almost to the brim with water and then tip in some glitter and close the lid tightly shut. The next step is to vigorously shake the jar to spin the glitter pieces around. Then ask your child to sit calmly and watch the glitter pieces swirl around and eventually settle. They can count to see how long it takes – or use a stop-watch or clock and record the length of time in a notebook. Keeping a record will make it more interesting – next time will the pieces take longer to come to a complete standstill or will it be quicker?

This activity can also be used as a time-out exercise – so much better than employing the use of a 'naughty step'. I also feel it's important to start this activity by asking your child to do the pouring of water, tipping in the glitter, screwing on the lid and shaking the pieces. It creates that intermediary step from busyness to stillness and will make it easier for them to sit and focus.

The Imaginary Camera

Encourage your child to notice what's going on around them and actively 'create memories' by pretending to have a camera in their mind that takes imaginary snapshots. They can notice all the good things as they happen – for example: a best friend pulling silly faces; a lovely birthday cake; jazzy decorations, etc. You can encourage them to do this by simply asking: *"Take a look around the room now and tell me, if you had a camera, what would you take a picture of?"* Find out which moments they would record and why.

MONTESSORI SILENCE GAME

This 'Silence Game' is something I used to teach the children in my school and it was astonishing to watch children, some as young as 3, become enthralled with the idea of achieving a state of complete silence and stillness. Dr Maria Montessori looked upon the benefits of the Silence Game as not just simply the absence of noise but more the creation of something special. Children's imaginations benefit from having the free space to think and this allows them to develop their creative talents. The relaxing effects of this exercise also reduce anxiety levels.

Learning how to take control of the body through the power of the mind is also the first step towards reducing impulsive behaviour as children develop a higher sense of awareness of what is happening around them. It helps to cut down on pushing, shoving, calling out loud, snatching toys and impatience. It is an integration of the whole being – mastery of mind over body, and it strengthens the will of the child to create this state for themselves. I recommend getting into the habit of playing it with your child and include a few friends too, for this activity has a greater impact the higher the number of children involved.

The Silence Game

1. Seat the children in a large circle on the floor.

2. Ensure that they are sitting in a position that's the most comfortable for them – not touching each other and with plenty of space between.

3. Tell them you are all going to be playing a game that consists of not moving at all! Explain that everyone is going to keep very, very quiet and very, very still. Every bit of their body needs to be still and quiet.

4. You'll be using your voice to lead the children in the direction of complete and utter stillness, so lower your voice so it sounds relaxing. Speak slowly and leave plenty of time between each instruction for those children who are slower to catch up. Towards the end you can start to whisper your instructions to highlight the fact that things are getting quieter and quieter.

Begin this process by saying:

- *Let's keep our feet very still, so even our toes become still.*
- Pause – wait for everyone to join in.
- *Now let's keep our legs very still.*
- *Now our bodies very still.*
- *Next our arms very, very still.*
- *Peaceful and quiet.*
- *Next, our hands very still, even our fingers, very still.*
- *Now our heads very still.*
- *Our mouths and eyes very still.*
- *Let's close our eyes so that even our eyelids are quite, quite still.*
- *All peaceful and quiet.*

If the earlier environment was quite noisy and exuberant, the sound of this silence and the sense of deep stillness in the air will be really intriguing and exciting for the children.

You can say:

- *Do you know what just happened?*
- Then answer your own question with: *We made a silence.*

The length of time that you play this game can be gradually extended as they become more proficient in their ability to keep totally still.

Have faith that gradually each child will join in with the game. To begin with you may find one child enjoys playing up and acting out in front of the group. Say nothing, for that would break the silence. Simply smile and allow the sound of your breathing to calm and relax the atmosphere.

Once your children are experienced at making a silence, you can progress to the next stage; listening out for sounds. Once a silence has been achieved, you can say:

- *Now we can begin to listen.*

After about 2 minutes of silence, you can go around the group one at a time and ask them what they heard during the Silence Game. One may have heard the sound of breathing or a clock ticking and another a bird tweeting outside or a train passing by.

If you usually play this game indoors, you can extend it by saying:

- *I wonder what would happen if we played this game outside? What sounds would we hear then?* And then next time you can move outside to play it again.

7

Psycho-sensory therapies

Psycho-sensory therapies are the newest and latest types of psychological therapeutic tools. Many developments have occurred in the field of neuro-science over the last ten years and there's a greater understanding of how anxiety and trauma are coded or stored in our bodies. Emotions, memories and experiences can be stored in a sensory way – which is why the smell of a perfume or home-cooked apple pie can trigger off an emotional response – even tears – depending on the connection or meaning that these have for you.

It's not uncommon for people to feel weepy or experience an emotional release after having a back massage, for example. The pressure applied to an aching shoulder is also releasing emotions that caused the muscle tension in the first place – be it a trauma such as a car crash or some other psychological tension such as sadness, frustration or anger.

It's also why more traditional talking therapies may not always work well at resolving problems such as PTSD – Post-Traumatic Stress Disorder. Sometimes the 'it's good to talk' method won't clear the problem effectively.

The most common forms of psycho-sensory therapies are:

- EMDR (Eye Movement Desensitisation and Reprocessing)
- TFT (Thought Field Therapy)
- EFT (Emotional Freedom Technique)
- Havening Techniques

These newer treatments can be 'content-free' – i.e. it's not necessary to talk about the events as it's not a conversational type of therapy. All that's required is to think about the unpleasant event and at the same time, follow a sequence of 'sensory input'. This can be rhythmic tapping, stroking of the arms or face, lateral movements of the eyes in quick succession, humming or counting out loud. Using sensory stimuli in this way can help to de-link the emotion from the memory, so while the person will still be able to remember the event (the time they got bitten by a dog), the feelings of panic and anxiety will have dissipated.

I've found these techniques particularly useful when helping children deal with episodes of school or online bullying. Several weeks or months after the event, it may not always be helpful to keep going round in circles talking about the past and so a psycho-sensory therapy may be more appropriate and helpful.

There will be those who point to the 'placebo effect' as being the reason for the success of these therapies, but I have worked with children as young as 3 and 4 years. At no time would I have explained to them that the technique we were about to do would rid them of their anxious feelings – we simply had a conversation and played a 'game'.

But in any event, in my view if a placebo effect has made someone feel better then it's still a 'win' and I wouldn't spend too much time searching for reasons to unpick the success of it. It's time to take advantage of the window of opportunity that the therapy has given you and move forward – quickly!

I'm going to feature two psycho-sensory therapies here: TFT and Havening. I've been trained in both and feel they're very effective. As well as erasing feelings of fear and anxiety, they are also useful as a means of simple relaxation and falling asleep more easily at night-time.

Both methods work in similar ways, but if I had to make a choice I'd be more inclined to use TFT tapping to take away feelings of stress in situations where I still wanted to feel focused and able to concentrate, e.g. sitting an exam or performing on stage. I'd use Havening if I wanted to feel less anxiety with a greater sense of relaxation and wellbeing. I have found Havening to be very, very relaxing. I recommend you practise using them on yourself before using them with your child so you can see what I mean.

Note: The instructions that I'm giving you here are for the relief of anxiety symptoms and for self-soothing. I would advise that you seek out a qualified therapist to tackle any more complicated traumas and more deep-seated emotional issues.

You will find many videos on YouTube that show how to use these techniques if you'd like to see them demonstrated more clearly.

THOUGHT FIELD THERAPY – THE TAPPING TECHNIQUE

Dr Roger Callahan, an eminent American psychologist, developed Thought Field Therapy in the 1980s to help people deal with all sorts of negative emotions. He discovered that tapping a specific sequence of acupuncture points in the body, whilst at the same time thinking about the problem (i.e. activating the thought processes and memories associated with the problem), can quickly reduce your levels of anxiety or stress.

This Tapping technique is ideal for dealing with feelings of stress, anxiety, lack of motivation or confidence. You can either teach your child how to use this technique or do it for them. Whenever my daughter struggled to fall asleep at night, she would call for me to come and 'tap' her as she lay in bed. All it usually took was a couple of rounds of the sequence, more commonly known as an algorithm, to have her drift off to sleep peacefully.

It's common to take a 'reading' using some sort of measurement tool at the start – see the example in Chapter 5. If you're using this technique for simple relaxation or as a sleep aid, or are still learning how to use it, there is no need to do this. It's only useful if you want to monitor how anxiety levels are reducing in response to a particular event or upcoming procedure.

You could take a reading at the start – and then again after the face tapping – and again at the end. But it's not always necessary and you may just want to follow the technique to soothe your child in the easiest way possible.

Refer to Figure 2 to locate the correct places to tap.

Figure 2

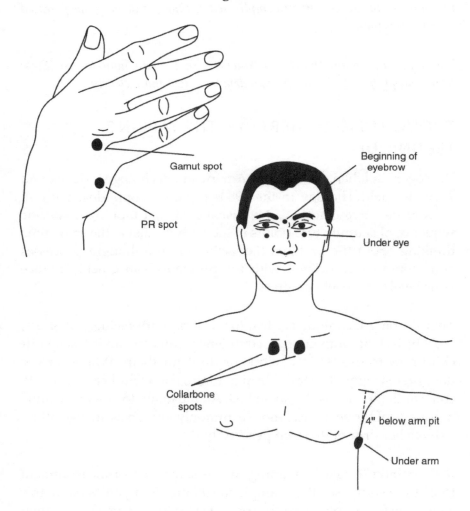

Gamut spot

PR spot

Beginning of
eyebrow

Under eye

Collarbone
spots

4" below arm pit

Under arm

TFT – Tapping Technique

Using two fingers on your more dominant hand, tap on the following points:

1. Five times between the eyebrows.

2. Five times under the eye.

3. Five times under the arm (*about 4 inches or 10cm below the armpit*).

4. Five times under the collarbone (*look for small hollows or spongy indentations just to the left and right of where the bones meet in the middle*).

5. Now pause. Take a reading from your measurement tool if you are using it.

6. Locate a dent on the back of your hand by the knuckle of the little finger. Tap here and *keeping your head very still*, look straight ahead and follow these instructions as you continue to tap all the time:

   • open your eyes

   • close your eyes

   • open your eyes and look down to the left

   • look down to the right

   • whirl your eyes around in one direction

   • whirl your eyes in the opposite direction

   • hum a few bars of any tune aloud

   • count aloud from one to five

   • hum the tune again

7. Repeat the process again using the first set of tapping points on the face.

8. Once you are happy with the change that has taken place, do a floor to ceiling eye roll (*hold your head level and move*

your eyes down to the floor and tap the gamut spot on the back of the hand as you roll them up to the ceiling).

Should you need further relief, simply repeat this exercise until you feel you have erased those unwanted feelings.

I recommend running through this technique each morning and each evening before bedtime. Encourage your child to do this in front of a mirror. The more it is used, the more powerful and quicker the effect will become and should you need to use it 'in an emergency situation' such as your child becoming startled by a wasp, spider or dog, then you'll know exactly what to do without having to think about the instructions too much.

TAPPING AFFIRMATIONS

Combining affirmations with your tapping skills will produce an even more powerful result – remember how I explained that the words that we speak and think to ourselves have an effect on the way the mind works.

It's very easy to get caught up with negative internal dialogue so no matter how positive you might feel about going out and getting top marks in that exam, those niggling worries often seem to have a way of worming their way in.

Begin tapping on the PR spot (side of hand) and say the following sentences out loud. I like this sequence of words as it builds up gradually to that point of success making it harder for your mind to argue with you.

Fill in the gaps with the most appropriate words for you:

- *I want to . . . .*
- *I can . . . .*
- *I will . . . .*
- *I am (or I do) . . . .*

Appropriate words could be:

- *feel calm and relaxed*
- *fall asleep easily*
- *remember all my spellings*
- *get top marks in the exam*
- *feel relaxed when I see a spider*
- *speak out with confidence*
- *feel happy and confident*

TAPPING AS FIRST AID

This shortcut version of the Tapping technique will prove invaluable as 'first aid' – for example, if your child gets feelings of panic visiting the dentist or having an injection. It may not be appropriate to run through the entire sequence when you're out and about in public.

Here are your short-cuts:

- Tap under the eye ten times.
- Tap on the side of the hand (on the karate chop PR spot) ten times.

Repeat as often as needed. I've taught these techniques to many children who have found tapping on these points useful during exam conditions.

> **TOP TIP:** *Next time you find yourself stuck in a traffic jam, gently tap the side of your hand as you hold the steering wheel. You'll notice how it helps to reduce those feelings of frustration – unfortunately, it won't clear the traffic any quicker and you won't reach your destination any faster, but you'll arrive feeling a lot less stressed!*

HAVENING

Dr Ronald Ruden is the creator of The Havening Techniques. Over the last three decades he has incorporated recent advances in neuro-science into new methods of healing. In his book, *When the Past is Always Present* (2010), he demonstrates how The Havening Techniques method, which uses sensory input (touch), can desensitise automatic responses of anxiety in the brain.

His twin brother, Dr Steven Ruden, has collaborated with him over the past ten years and The Havening Techniques therapy is becoming more widely recognised with research studies being carried out at King's College, London.[3]

The technique that I'll be describing here is for you to use with your child as a means of soothing and calming. If your child has experienced a more severe trauma or suffers from a psychological disorder, I recommend you seek help from a suitably qualified practitioner to help you work through the problem.

As before, if you'd like extra guidance, you'll be able to find videos on YouTube with demonstrations on how to follow this technique. I particularly recommend those featuring Paul McKenna.

As well as sensory input – in the form of stroking and touching – you'll be asking your child to visualise themselves doing simple activities. In the following example, I've used *walking on a sandy beach, stroking a favourite pet's back* and *jumping on a trampoline*. You can use whatever activities you think might suit your child – for example:

- *pedalling along on their bicycle;*
- *stirring cake mixture in a mixing bowl with a wooden spoon;*
- *brushing their hair with a large hairbrush;*
- *walking through the woods;*
- *swimming backstroke in a swimming pool.*

I recommend you practise using this technique on yourself before teaching it to your child. You'll get a better understanding of how to use it and it will also give you an opportunity to experience feelings of relaxation at the touch of your fingertips.

Self-Havening

1. In a seated position, cross your arms in an X across your chest and begin running your fingertips down the sides of your arms in a stroking action.

2. Close your eyes and now clear your mind and imagine that you are *walking along a nice sandy beach on a summer's day*. With each footstep that you take in the sand, count out loud from the number one to the number 20.

3. Then open your eyes, but keep stroking the sides of your arms.

4. Keeping your head very still, move your eyes to look to the right. Then look to the left. Then to the right again – then back to the left. Repeat this lateral movement of the eyes from side to side about ten times.

5. Now close your eyes again and imagine that you are *sitting with your favourite pet and you begin stroking its back*. With each long, slow stroke you can again count out loud from the number one to the number 20. Keep stroking the sides of your arms throughout.

6. Then open your eyes and repeat the instructions in No. 4.

7. Now close your eyes once more and this time imagine that you are *jumping on a trampoline*. With each bounce that you take, count out loud from the number one to the number 20.

8. Open your eyes and stop stroking your arms.

9. You've just flooded your brain with delta waves that will increase your serotonin levels. The bad, unwanted feelings will have reduced in their intensity. Repeat the process if you feel you need to work on them some more.

You can find out more on the website: www.havening.org/.

Visualisation techniques

ABOUT NEURO-LINGUISTIC PROGRAMMING (NLP)

In this chapter I'm going to be introducing you to guided visualisation techniques that are commonly associated with Neuro-
Linguistic Programming. Despite its complicated sounding name,
NLP is really quite simple and the principles help us to understand
how our mind works and how information randomly absorbed from
our environment creates our thoughts which go on to determine
our behaviour.

Developed in the early 1970s in California by Richard Bandler
and John Grinder, NLP is becoming recognised as one of the
most effective psychological methods. It's widely used today in
the fields of communication, commerce, personal development,
psychotherapy, education and medicine. Learning NLP will enable
you to have more control over your thoughts and this will help you
to change the way you feel and how you behave, more easily.

I've written more about NLP in my book, *Fix Your Life with NLP*,
published by Simon & Schuster. You'll find details on my website.

LEARNING HOW TO CHANGE MENTAL IMAGES

Think back to the last time you watched a scary movie at the cinema
or on TV. It didn't matter that you knew it was only make-believe
did it? Simply watching scary images can trigger off palpitations,
sweaty palms, tingling sensations in the hands and feet or sick
feelings in the stomach area. Some of us will even scream out loud.

Because we know that this happens, it tells us that our minds can't distinguish between a real or imagined event – whatever the mind is watching or seeing, the body will respond to.

One of the quickest ways to change anxious feelings in the body is to become immediately aware of the images that accompany the thoughts and change them too. Here's an exercise you can carry out with your child to help them practise how to do this.

Magic TV Control Exercise

1. Find a quiet place for you and your child to run through this exercise. Explain to your child that scary feelings are created by scary thoughts inside their imagination and that you're going to teach them how to change these thoughts using a Magic TV Control.

2. I feel it's a good idea to practise this technique with an image that doesn't cause your child any distress so simply ask them to think of their best friend – or their favourite TV character.

3. Now ask them to describe the image that they're seeing inside their imagination. What does this friend or character look like? How tall are they? What colour is their hair? What clothes are they wearing? And what about the shoes on their feet? Fill in all the details.

4. Now, using the Magic TV Control, tell them to change that image very slowly, step by step. Start with the colours – could they change the colour of their best friend's hair to bright green, for example?

5. And how about their clothes? Could they change the clothes for something different – say, a football kit, a firefighter's uniform or a pair of stripey pyjamas?

6. And don't forget the shoes. Would it be funny to put them in a pair of yellow wellingtons or clown's shoes with a bell on the end? Take your time to make suggestions about all

the details that could be changed to make the friend or TV character look completely different.

7. Next, can they make all the colours in this image really bright and bold? Ask them to use a button on that imaginary TV control inside their mind to do this.

8. And what about the sounds in this image? Could they make this friend or character sing a song? Can they turn up the volume to make it louder? Can they turn it down to make it softer?

9. Can they imagine them skipping and dancing around the room in a ridiculous fashion? And if they did this, can they imagine what their friend would say? Would they be cross? Or would they laugh out loud?

10. Continue playing around with this image. Make the colours brighter and bolder and then drain them out so they're hardly visible. Make the sounds louder and then turn the volume down so the sounds are really soft. Make the moving image as still as a statue. Notice the expression on the face of the person in this image. Are they happy or cross that your child is playing around with them like this?

11. Then, at the touch of a button on the Magic TV Control, your child can quickly turn this character back to look just how they should look. Finish up by noticing the expression on the face of this character – are they happier to be looking their usual self once more? Or did they prefer to dress up and act out?

12. Children often find this exercise very amusing – so if your child starts to grin or laugh out loud, you'll know that they are able to access the images inside their mind and also to change them.

13. Finish off by telling your child that they're very good at playing around with pictures inside their imagination and that being able to do this will help them in the future when they're feeling anxious.

CHANGING SCARY PICTURES

Scary feelings are usually accompanied by a worrying image and being able to change this image will change the feelings. Before following this exercise, you'll need to have taught your child how to use the Magic TV Control, details of which are given in the previous exercise.

Exercise

1. Ask your child to conjure up the scary image or thought and describe it to you. This may be something such as an imaginary scary monster under the bed or perhaps something more real, e.g. feeling anxious about going to school the next day, in case a particular child teases them, or perhaps they're worried they'll score zero in a spelling or maths test.

2. Ask them to describe it to you in detail. And then tell them that it's time to change that image.

3. Turn the colour down on those pictures making them less bright. The fainter the colours the better, so keep going to get the brightness down.

4. And if there's any dialogue, music or sounds that go with that image, tap the appropriate button on the TV control to turn the volume right down.

5. Continue adjusting the picture in this way – drain all the colour out of it, making it black and white and removing any traces of sound.

6. Next, start shrinking it right down till it's nothing more than a dot.

7. Now that you're left with a dot, your child can choose what to do with it. Either delete it completely by pressing one of the buttons, or be a bit more creative with it. Perhaps they'll prefer to pick it up in their hands and throw it out of the window – far, far away into the distance. Encourage them to do anything they'd like to do with it to banish it from their thoughts entirely.

8. Then press the 'off' button on this imaginary TV control. After all, if you were watching something on a real TV that you weren't enjoying, you'd switch it off, wouldn't you?

You can finish by asking your child to put a good picture in place instead. What's their favourite TV show? Conjure up a new image that will enable them to relax and feel better.

Would they prefer an image of a super-hero or perhaps the family pet to keep them happy? Or even an image of themselves doing a favourite activity such as riding their bicycle or playing football – anything that makes them feel really, really good and happy.

Note: A variation of this exercise would be to ask your child to draw a picture of their scary thought or nightmare. Then they could change the details in the picture by drawing smiley faces on monsters or doing whatever they need to do to make the picture a friendly one.

CREATING A VOLUME CONTROL

Not only are we constantly hearing sounds around us, but we're also hearing the little voices or sounds inside our minds all day long. This is called our 'internal dialogue' – it's not uncommon for people to doubt that they have one and if you're not sure about the existence of yours, then silently ask yourself the question "where is my internal dialogue?" and you'll locate it.

It's useful to firstly, become aware of the existence of this voice and secondly, to have the ability to change it or switch it off altogether. This voice does not always serve us well – it contributes to our worrying, reminding us that we'll probably fail all our exams; it unhelpfully tells us that our appearance isn't too great each time we look in a mirror and if we've heard some harsh comments from friends or teachers at school, our internal dialogue will insist on playing this on repeat for many hours, if not days, after the event.

Even when we read online comments, we automatically give them a voice and along with it comes an intonation. We put our own personal spin on what we read, which is why it's common to receive a text message and inadvertently give it a slightly distorted sense and meaning:

- *You sent me a horrible text . . .*
- *No, I was only joking, I was trying to be nice . . .*
- *Well, it didn't sound like you were . . .*

Note the use of the word 'sound' in that last statement when in fact, because this was a text message, the only sound you could have heard is the one you gave it yourself!

Helping your child to become acquainted with their own internal dialogue and have the ability to alter and change it will help them to deal with hurtful comments and their own negative thoughts much more easily.

Note: Some of you may be questioning the need for a 'Volume Control' as, naturally, there ought to be a button on the TV Control in the previous exercise that can change the internal dialogue too. I've created this as a separate exercise because I think it's more helpful for those circumstances where there are no readily available images. For example, have you ever had an irritating telephone conversation with someone and got stuck with their words in your mind for ages afterwards? Not having had a face-to-face meeting means you may not be 'seeing' anything and that's why this exercise concentrates purely on the sounds being heard.

Exercise

Part 1

1. Point out to your child some of the different controls that can be found around the house – for example, a light switch that flicks on and off or perhaps a dimmer switch that rotates round. Some switches are dials, others are levers and some have buttons like the control of a television.

2. Ask your child to close their eyes for a few moments to take a really good look at the volume control that controls the sounds inside their mind.

3. What colour is it? And what about the shape – is it round, square or long?

4. Does it have a dial – or a button, a slider or a digital control?

5. Can your child notice which setting it's on? Does it have numbers one to ten or higher? Does it have the words 'low, medium, high'?

6. Ask your child to open their eyes now and encourage them to draw a picture of this volume control so they get a really good sense of how it looks. Younger children can describe it to you so you can draw it – and older children (teenagers) can describe it in the form of notes if they prefer, perhaps recording the information on a mobile phone.

Note: if your child struggles to imagine a volume control, then prompt them by saying 'If you did have one, I wonder what yours would look like.' or 'If you could choose to have any kind of volume control you wanted, what kind do you think would do the job best?'

Part 2

1. Explain to your child that now they have a good sense of what their volume control looks like, they'll be able to test it out and play around with it.

2. Ask them to imagine a song playing silently in their mind – this could be the Happy Birthday song or the theme tune to one of their favourite TV shows or another song they really like.

3. Now that they can hear it playing, ask them to turn the volume up a little bit louder. And then louder still. Pause to allow them time to do this and encourage them to notice what it is they need to do on this special control of theirs to change the volume.

4. Now can they turn the volume down, so it's a little bit quieter. And then quieter still – so perhaps it's nothing more than a whisper.

5. And now ask them to turn the volume back up. A little bit louder – and a little bit louder again. Louder still . . . and how about so, so loud that if they were really playing this song at this volume at home, the neighbours would most probably hear it; the dog would start barking and the baby would begin to cry! (Add in your own details to make this amusing.)

6. And now they can turn the volume down to an acceptable level – before switching it off completely.

7. Have a discussion by asking them to describe the steps they had to take to turn the volume up and then back down again. They can refer to the picture they drew earlier.

Note: I've designed this control to adjust the volume of the internal dialogue, but you can also distort the voice into a more comical one, e.g. Mickey Mouse, a character from Spongebob Squarepants or any other voice they find amusing.

Changing a bully's voice into a ridiculous sounding one will take the sting or emotion out of the hurtful words that are being heard. Your child will most likely be able to laugh about the criticism or insult and shrug it off all the easier.

STOP THAT THOUGHT

Creating a 'stop button' is another useful technique for getting rid of repetitive thoughts. A bit like an 'ear worm' – the term used to describe a persistent piece of music that gets stuck in your head. I've taken to calling thoughts that get stuck in your mind a 'thought worm'. Sometimes this internal dialogue is simply annoying and we'll find the negativity draining, but other thoughts can have more serious connotations. It's possible to feel as if certain ideas are invading our thinking space and almost telling us what to do and how to behave. This is a common feature of obsessive-compulsive disorders and obsessional thoughts – those that seem to be telling us to behave in a certain way, even though we know we just don't want to.

As I like to point out, it's useful to remember that we do not act on every single thought that comes into our mind. We regularly have thoughts that we simply ignore. For example, if a traffic warden slaps a ticket on my car, out of frustration the thought that may come into my mind is *"Oh, I could murder that traffic warden!"*. But of course, I'm not going to do any such thing – it's just a thought, nothing more, and it's a thought I can easily ignore. The thought is not going to control me.

In fact there are many thoughts that pop into our minds each and every day that we find very easy to ignore. I know that *'I must do the ironing'* or *'I should do my tax return'* are particularly easy to dismiss.

And I bet your child also has these kind of thoughts – how about '*I should do my homework*' or '*I need to pack my school bag for the morning*' or even '*I should go upstairs to get ready for bed*'. Kids find it very easy to shrug these off.

And in just the same way, it's possible to learn how to banish unwanted, annoying or scary thoughts for good. These thoughts have no great power over us – only the power that we give them. And what we give, we can also take away.

You can do the following exercise with your child and they can use paper and coloured pens if they'd like to. I often recommend drawing pictures because it's a clear indication of whether your child has a good idea of what they're creating. Older children and teenagers may not want to draw pictures and I think it would be just as effective if they were to jot down hand-written details or make notes on their mobile phone.

Exercise

1. Explain to your child that they have an opportunity to design a special 'stop button': an imaginary button that can be pressed quickly to stop any unwanted thoughts that may attempt to weasel their way into their mind.

2. Ask your child to close their eyes and take a few moments to imagine what this special button could look like.

3. Give prompts to help your child with their design: *Now, I don't know if your button will be a round button, a square button or maybe even a triangular button. But I do know that you'll be able to start seeing it clearly now.*

4. *And how about the colour? I don't know if you're going to choose a red button, a blue button, green or even yellow or orange. I wonder what colour you'll be thinking of?*

5. Continue to gently guide your child in their design, ensuring that they have plenty of time to dream and imagine. Encourage them to tell you out-loud what it is that they're seeing and make a note of the details that they give you.

6. Then you can ask them to open their eyes and draw a picture of the button that they visualised in their imagination.

7. Sit with them as they draw their picture – and perhaps you'll want to draw one for yourself too.

8. When the drawings are finished, explain to your child that next time they sense these thoughts or words coming into their mind, all they have to do is press the STOP button.

9. Practise now – ask your child to close their eyes once more and imagine pressing that STOP button hard. Ask them to explain to you once more exactly what it is they have to do to get those thoughts to stop and go away.

10. When you've tested it out a few times and your child is happy, stick the picture up on the wall or fridge where it can be seen. In future, whenever their thinking is starting to spiral downwards, you can call out 'Let's STOP'.

11. With this visual image in their mind, your child will find it very much easier to gain control over their emotions.

Note: If at any time in the future you find the STOP button doesn't work, then it's a case of going back to the drawing board. Tell your child that the button needs fixing. During the visualisation process, guide them through some changes – along the lines of:

- *Would it be better if the button were bigger?*

- *Do you need to change the shape?*

- *What about the colour – would you like to change this at all?*

- *How about turning the button into a handle or lever that you pull down instead?*

- *Would it be better if it made a sound?*

- *How about the sound of a ship's foghorn or a cow mooing? Or a voice shouting STOP? And if so, whose voice? A super-hero perhaps?*

- You can research some sounds and voices on the internet and ask your child to choose one.

I also find the phrase 'a train of thought' useful to think about. We can imagine our thoughts as a train coming into our mind from the left side or the right side of our head and then deciding whether to engage with them or not. Imagine the middle of your head as the station – when you have control of your thoughts, you can choose to allow them to stop at the station (in which case, you'll take notice of them) or turn them into an express train that speeds right the way through without stopping (in which case, you'll ignore them).

If your child prefers this analogy, use this instead.

SPINNING ANXIOUS FEELINGS AWAY

Anxiety can be felt rushing through our bodies in many different ways: our hearts pound away in our chests, there's a tightness in the throat, a sick or sinking feeling in the stomach or even pins and needles in the hands or legs.

In order for us to 'feel' a feeling it has to keep moving – the energy has to keep travelling throughout our body. Let me explain: if I came over to you and stamped on your foot hard, you'd be in pain. And if I came and did it again, you'd feel pain again.

But interestingly, if I came over to you and placed my foot on top of your foot and just kept it there, after the initial reaction, you'd stop feeling the pain. Your foot would habituate to the weight of my foot and would no longer experience it there.

It's the same if I were to stick a small needle in your arm and quickly remove it. You'd certainly feel pain. But if I were to insert the needle and just hold it there, again, you'd habituate to the feeling and no longer feel it in the same way.

In order to experience feelings of anxiety, we know that the feelings have to be moving or vibrating through the body as they travel around because if they were static we'd stop noticing them quite quickly. Phrases such as 'butterflies in the stomach' aptly describe what's going on.

Good feelings tend to travel in one direction and bad feelings in another – and being able to locate the direction in which they're moving will give you the opportunity to not only change the direction of travel but also shift the feeling from anxiety to good feelings.

Exercise

1. Next time your child is feeling anxious, ask them to become aware of whereabouts in the body they are experiencing those feelings. If they find it difficult to pinpoint the region, I often joke by saying *"Are you feeling it at the end of your nose? Or perhaps in your big toe?"* This often produces some laughter – and also clarity, leading to a response of *"no, it's in my tummy"*.

2. Ask your child to use a finger to point to the area where the anxious feelings are and then to indicate the direction of travel. The anxious feelings could be travelling around in small circles clockwise or anti-clockwise – or they could be running from the top of the head down to the feet and back up again. They should continue to point and track the movement of the feeling with their finger.

3. Now ask your child to give those unwanted feelings a colour – any colour they feel accurately represents the way they are experiencing them right now.

4. This next step might seem a strange one – but stick with this. Using your hands, pretend to pull out that anxious feeling out of your child's body. This can be quite funny. Now that you have the 'feeling' in your hands, make a big performance of turning it around and flipping it over.

5. Now, you can insert it back into your child's body – and because you've flipped it around, the feeling will now start to travel in the opposite direction. So if it's spinning in a clockwise direction, it will now start to spin in an anti-clockwise direction. If it's travelling from the head down to the feet, it will now travel up the body instead. All the feelings will be moving in the opposite way.

6. Ask your child to use their finger once more to point to the feeling and track the direction of travel again. Encourage them to notice how different it feels right now. Because we've reversed everything about the old feeling of anxiety, this new feeling will now be a positive, happy, confident one.

7. Your child can now change the colour of this new feeling – so if it were red before, it now might become blue instead.

8. The final step is to speed up the movement of the feeling – tell your child to get it to spin or move ten times faster than it ever did before. This will increase the new positive feelings all the more.

9. Lastly, ask your child to think of something that makes them feel good at the same time – a favourite friend, the family pet, chocolate ice-cream. These new thoughts will help the new positive feelings to grow and expand.

I once worked with a child that described his feelings of anxiety as *"black, wriggly worms swimming around my tummy"*. I'm sure you can see how by changing the submodalities of this image by using this spinning technique I was able to help him enormously.

IN TWO MINDS

We all know what it's like to struggle to change a habit or behaviour when there's a 'secondary gain' or fear lurking in the background that's determined to keep us stuck in our old, more established pattern of behaviour.

How many of us would like to lose weight but on the other hand, don't want to give up our daily latte and muffin? And who would like to get really fit and go to the gym five times a week, but on the other hand doesn't want to get out of bed an hour earlier each morning, or arrive home later from work?

I've given some pretty obvious examples there, but you can see how this would work if your child suffers from a fear of the dark and enjoys coming into your bed each night as a consequence. Snuggling up in bed with Mum or Dad becomes the bigger driver – the incentive to ditch that fear of the dark is no longer uppermost in the mind.

Let's take another example: on the one hand your child really loves performing or singing but on the other hand is too terrified to stand on stage in front of an audience. Playing small is going to be the more preferable course of action.

Perhaps your child would really like to go on sleepovers with friends but the safety and security of staying at home in their own bed is pushing them into avoidance mode.

And when one child in the family receives more time and attention as a result of having their fear or phobia, there's likely to be more anxiety about what will happen if they lose the problem, rather than if they keep the problem for ever. At least, they know and understand their fear or anxiety and have probably created coping strategies for living with it.

Success becomes much harder to achieve when there's a little bit of an internal struggle going on. It's good to have a discussion with your child and point out that these negative feelings are serving a purpose – they are trying to protect your child and their intention is good. So even though it feels as if they are being pulled in two different directions, both sides only want the best for them. However, these hyper-vigilant feelings are having a sabotaging effect and are holding your child back from achieving what they'd really like to. It's a good idea to always keep in mind the ultimate goal – what would your child really like to have happen?

- Go to school feeling relaxed and eager to see their friends.
- Perform on stage feeling happy and confident.
- Sleep through the night knowing they are safe and secure.

Encourage your child to see that it's natural to feel that 'on the one hand' they'd like something to change but 'on the other hand' they'd also like things to stay the same.

This following exercise will help to get both parts in agreement to making some changes.

Exercise

1. Have a conversation with your child and help them to identify any worrying thoughts, doubts or beliefs they may have about changing their anxious behaviour. It may help to write these down on a large piece of paper – or even draw pictures.

2. Once you have done this, stand in front of your child and ask them to place both hands out in front of them with palms facing up to the ceiling. Tell your child to imagine the part of them that would like to act in the more positive way in their right hand. And then the negative part, the bit of them that worries, in their left hand.

Example: the part that would like to go to the park to play with friends in their right hand. And the part of them that is petrified of dogs, and wants to avoid going to the park, in their left hand.

3. Ask your child to look at the left hand for a few moments and try to visualise an image of themselves feeling worried about whatever the problem is, on top of their palm.

4. Then ask them to look into the right hand and see themselves behaving differently, with confidence, feeling happy – able to conquer their fears Again, ask them to conjure up an image in the palm of their hand.

5. As they look into each hand in turn, ask your child what they think the positive intention of each part is. Continue asking these questions until it becomes clear that both parts only want the same thing – to keep your child safe and secure.

6. Keep running through this process even if it feels a little strange to begin with. Doing this will create changes in

confidence and self-belief. Too often we begin to dislike the part of us that holds us back from achieving what we'd like to achieve and this exercise helps us to make 'friends' with the seemingly negative part. It's like calling a truce – accepting that the struggle can begin to stop from now on.

7. Now as they look down into the empty space between their two out-stretched hands, ask them to imagine that they can see a 'super-part' emerging. A super-part that has the resources to keep both sides happy and still be able to move forward successfully.

Example: using the earlier example of being too afraid to visit the park to play with friends because of a fear of dogs, this super-part may come up with suggestions such as: visiting another family member who has a dog twice a week for 5 minutes, so they can gradually get used to being in the company of dogs. Or maybe going to the park with a trusted adult or friend who they feel will keep them safe to begin with.

8. As they continue to look down into the empty space between their hands encourage them to keep seeing that new super-part emerge. This will be solution, the answer to their problem. They may not see it clearly to begin with, but by planting the suggestion into their mind that they can and will resolve this issue, it will become easier for them to do so.

9. Now, moving quickly, ask them to cup both hands together to allow those two separate parts in the left and in the right hands to merge with the super-part and become one entity.

10. Ask them to raise their hands up to their chest to, allow this new 'super-part' to become fully absorbed and integrated as a new part of their personality. Encourage your child to close their eyes as they do this and to really enjoy this moment of seeing how their new future will look from now on, with every bit of their body in agreement.

Help your child to continue practising this technique and you'll find that gradually their feelings of internal conflict will simply begin to disappear.

ANCHORING

Feelings, sensations and responses in our bodies can be triggered off by all sorts of things and not just by our thoughts. *Anchoring* is the word used to describe the link between a trigger or stimulus and a response. In other words, something in our environment – it could be a sound, a smell, a piece of music, a thought – triggers off a reaction in us. This reaction could be happiness, sadness, nervousness, anxiety, confidence, elation – responses that just happen automatically without you having much control over them, unless you become aware of what's happening.

Anchors are all around us: we can hear a specific piece of music and find ourselves filled with emotion and for many of us, the music from a passing ice-cream van will instantly trigger childhood memories.

Smells can produce particularly strong responses: the smell of a certain perfume can remind you of the excitement of a first date. But then again, the smell of a food that once gave you food poisoning can be enough to set off a similarly bad response.

It's no surprise that many people will claim their mother's apple pie or Victoria sponge cake is the best in the world, for it's not simply the taste that produces this response but the feelings of love, comfort, safety and security it was served with.

NLP anchoring is one of the most popular NLP techniques. It's easy to do and extremely powerful. It will give you the control to put yourself in the kind of states you'd like to be in, at the push of a button.

This link was originally discovered by Ivan Pavlov, the famous Russian scientist who carried out an experiment with his dogs. Each time the dogs were given some food, their mouths would begin to salivate in response. Pavlov decided to ring a bell each time he fed the dogs, so that pretty soon the dogs would begin to associate the ringing of the bell with food. He then discovered that the sound of the bell was all that was needed to trigger off the salivation in the dogs, even if it wasn't feeding time and there was no food around for them to see or smell. Their bodies produced an automatic response (i.e. saliva) even if they were not hungry.

In NLP the same principles are used to create anchors but this time, they can be done deliberately to make links and associations with desirable states, rather than leaving us to cope with unwanted anchors that have occurred in our lives haphazardly.

Creating anchors in this way is a valuable skill that can enable us to change feelings from an undesired state to a desired one – from stress to feelings of relaxation; from anger to calm; from self-doubt to confidence; from sadness to happiness.

In the following exercises, I'm going to show you how to establish an anchor for feelings of confidence and also feelings of calmness in your child. As I mentioned, an 'attachment' is made in the mind between a particular set of feelings and a stimulus and this is done deliberately.

Commonly, good thoughts and feelings are encouraged to the forefront of the mind and at the same time, the person is asked to squeeze the middle finger on their more dominant hand, against the thumb. And this creates a kind of switch or trigger for inducing those more desirable feelings at some future moment. For example, if your child is due to perform on stage and has been suffering from feelings of nervousness, then it would be very useful to set up a positive anchor so that just before they walk on stage, they can squeeze those fingers together once more and release a shot of feelgood chemicals into their bodies – just as Pavlov's dogs salivated.

I've used this technique with children many times and I find it works really well.

Exercise: Creating a Confidence Anchor

Note: You'll be asking your child to create a 'switch' to trigger good feelings. This is usually done by squeezing the thumb and middle finger on the dominant hand together. If your child finds this awkward to do, you can ask them to squeeze their hand into a fist instead.

If your child struggles to conjure up clear memories inside their imagination, remind them that it's a skill they will gradually learn – a bit like learning how to read silently inside your head. To begin with it was tricky but gradually all of us learn how to do this.

An alternative to creating the image inside their mind is to ask them to draw pictures instead. They'll then be able to stick the pictures on their bedroom wall and these will serve as additional reminders.

1. Find somewhere comfortable and quiet to sit with your child and encourage them to start feeling relaxed – perhaps by blowing three long slow breaths into an imaginary paper bag.

2. Ask your child to remember a time in the past when they felt really confident and happy. Try to come up with examples where they felt the kind of good feelings they'd like to be feeling right now.

For example, if they're experiencing feelings of nervousness about going to a friend's birthday party, can you remind them of a time when they went to a party and had a great time? Do try to come up with times in the past when your child truly did feel extra special and confident.

3. Ask your child to close their eyes and take themselves back to that good time. Tell them to see all that they saw, hear all that they heard and feel the good, happy feelings that they felt back then. Perhaps they could describe the scene for you. What was so special and good about this moment?

4. In order to help them create this image, ask them to make the picture a bit bigger – to turn the colours up brighter,

bolder, stronger, and if there are any sounds in this memory of theirs, to turn the volume up louder. *Note: refer to the earlier Magic TV Control exercise as this will help.*

5. Then ask them to make that picture even bigger and bring it closer to themselves.

6. Can they see themselves in that image, having fun? This is a time in the past when they felt truly happy, confident and successful.

7. As the feelings associated with this memory become stronger, ask them to squeeze together the thumb and middle finger on their dominant hand. Squeeze them together tightly, capturing all of those good, good feelings.

8. Hold for a minute and then release the fingers and relax the hand. They can then open their eyes once more.

9. Now choose a couple more examples of times in the past when your child felt really confident and successful – talk about these times with your child. Perhaps it was when a teacher at school praised them for a good piece of work – perhaps when they managed to ride their bike without falling off for the first time – perhaps when they swam a length of the local pool when they had doubted themselves capable. Or can you think of a time in the past when something funny happened and they just couldn't stop laughing?

10. Talk about these events and pick two more scenarios. Repeat Step 3, encouraging them to recall that memory with vivid colours, sounds and feelings. And as they do, ask them to squeeze that thumb and middle finger (or fist) once more, capturing all of those good feelings there.

Running through this exercise several times will ensure that the 'confident anchor' becomes more powerful – repetition is the key to getting this anchor to work even better.

Tell your child that they'll be able to use this anchor switch every time they need to feel a little more confident – perhaps when they're walking onto the football pitch to play a match, reading out loud in class, walking into an exam room or just going to play at a friend's house.

All they need to do is squeeze that thumb and middle finger together once more and their body will automatically be flooded with feelgood chemicals making it easier for them to handle the situation.

You can help them to intensify this feelgood anchor by encouraging them to squeeze those fingers again each time something good happens – e.g. they're eating chocolate ice-cream or laughing at their favourite TV show.

CREATING OTHER ANCHORS

Now that you have a blueprint for creating an anchor, you'll be able to help your child create other anchors for different emotions.

For example, you can create a 'Calm Anchor' to induce more helpful feelings in place of exam room nerves or when struggling to fall asleep. Choose relaxing moments from the past to attach to the anchor: these could be lying in a warm relaxing bath, lying on the sofa surrounded by comfy cushions whilst watching a favourite TV show or a time in the past when you all relaxed on a warm, sunny beach.

As before, when needing a boost of calming, relaxing feelings, just squeezing the thumb and middle finger will trigger off these feelings once more.

Note: If you decide to create more than one anchor, I recommend using a different hand, so, for example, you could have a calm, relaxing anchor on the left hand and a confident, energetic anchor on the right hand.

SUPERSIZE YOUR CONFIDENCE

There will be occasions when your child will need an extra shot of confidence, for example: auditions, music recitals, stage performances and interviews and this technique will be ideal.

Exercise

1. Create a circle on the floor or ground using a piece of chalk; a long piece of cord, ribbon or string; or a plastic hula-hoop.

2. Whilst standing outside the circle, ask your child to think about the challenging situation that's coming up in the future and discuss it. Ask them to take a few moments to consider it. Who will be there? Where will it be? How much time will there be? What is the desired outcome?

3. Encourage them to think about the resources or skills they'll need. For example, an audition or stage performance requires a bit of star quality; a job interview requires you to be confident and able to think freely; an exam or sports event may require you to be calm and focused.

4. Position your child so they're standing with a good, confident posture or pose. A super-hero pose with legs apart and hands on hips is good for this. Ask them to have a good picture in their mind of how they'd like the event to go. They can describe it to you, with prompts if needed.

5. Now, ask them to recall a time in the past when they had all the resources they'll need at this upcoming event. So even if the stage performance is their first one, perhaps they sang a song loudly or danced enthusiastically during a game at a friend's birthday party. Likewise for a job interview, you could encourage them to recall a time in the past when they confidently explained to a relative or family friend what they'd like to do when they leave school. For an exam, remember a time in the past when an exam or class test did go well.

6. When all the resources that will be needed have been identified, ask your child to step into the magic circle, close their eyes and relive that time again. Talk it through with them, encouraging them to see what they saw, hear what they heard, feel what they felt and make that image in their mind grow and grow. As the picture grows so too will the strength of their feelings. You can embellish this image by asking them to turn the colours up more brightly and the sounds more loudly – a bit like having their own personal TV control.

7. Ask them to squeeze together either their fist (for younger children) or their thumb and middle finger on the dominant hand (better for older children and teens) to 'capture' all of those good feelings. Do this for at least 30 seconds.

8. Next, they can relax the hand and step out of the circle.

9. Then, ask them to think of another feeling or resource they'll need to handle this future situation well. Search back through the memories once more to remember a time in the past when they had exactly that resource.

10. Ask your child to step back into the circle again and run through Steps 6 and 7 once more, with this new memory.

11. Once finished, let them step back out of the circle and open their eyes.

12. Tell your child to relax and now suggest that they think of a friend (real or imagined) that they'd like to have alongside them as a support at this future event. It could even be the family pet or a favourite TV character.

13. Get them to hop back into the circle and run through Steps 6 and 7 once more with all the good feelings that having this imaginary buddy alongside them gives them.

14. Let them come back out of the circle.

15. Once you have gathered together and anchored all the resources and feelings your child will need or want for this event, get them to jump back into your circle once more.

16. Now, with eyes closed, ask them to visualise that future event going just the way they'd like it to. Describe the event from start to finish for them as they imagine it in their mind. As you do this, ask them to squeeze their fist (if they used it first time around) or thumb and middle finger and automatically those good, good feelings will flood their body as they mentally rehearse the upcoming challenging situation. Fill in the details so they can see what they'll be wearing; see the other people there; ask them to notice their confident posture, composure, tone of voice, feelings of inner strength – not forgetting, of course, the relaxed smile on their face – the sign that tells them all is going well.

17. They can imagine the circle has a colour – a good strong colour – one that represents confidence and success to them.

18. As they stand in the circle with eyes closed, ask them to imagine this colour rising up in a mist all around them. As it travels up, they can imagine it swirling around all the way to the top of their head and beyond.

19. Why not add a bit of stardust to it for good measure? And encourage your child to really enjoy this moment, with everything going just the way they'd like it to.

20. Then they can open their eyes, relax their hand and step out of the circle.

The more this gets practised, the stronger the feelings of confidence will be. Then when they experience the future event for real, they can either squeeze that fist or thumb and middle finger together again, and all these resourceful feelings will flood their body once more. This will enable them to handle the situation in just the way they want – with extra confidence!

YOUR BRIGHT, NEW, SHINY FUTURE

Many of the techniques that I've explained here focus on taking bad feelings away. When someone has been feeling anxious or depressed for some time, it can feel strange to let go of those feelings.

While they may be unpleasant and unwanted, after a time the body habituates to these feelings and they begin to feel normal – in fact, they are the person's 'normal' way of being.

Simply deleting them will leave a gap or an empty space and when this starts to feel strange, the mind will want to bring back the old feelings, for *something* is better than nothing. It's why you might hear someone say that they tried a therapy or a few strategies to get rid of anxiety and while it worked to begin with, it then 'wore off'. Often the problem is that the new way of thinking and feeling had not been sufficiently embedded.

Here's an outline of a technique that you can adapt to suit your child's circumstances:

Exercise

1. To begin with your child will need to take a few moments to relax in a comfortable place – this could be as they lie in bed, relax on the sofa or even as they lie in the bath. You could even do this exercise outside in the garden as they relax under a tree. It could even be as they sit in the back of the car as you're parked up waiting for someone. There are often plenty of good opportunities to do this throughout the day – never waste a moment.

2. As your child closes their eyes, ask them to imagine themselves sitting in a cinema with the huge screen in front of them.

3. Today they will be watching a very special movie – this is going to be a film of their bright, new, shiny future.

4. Decide on an appropriate title for this film. And what about a soundtrack? Is there a favourite piece of music that you could use? Something that will help your child to feel really happy, motivated and confident about their future.

5. Let the film begin. This is a short film of a time in the future when your child can see everything going just the way they'd like it to. So, this could be an audition, interview

or stage performance. It could be a trip to the dentist, a medical appointment or a hospital stay. Choose an event that has been worrying your child in the past.

6. As they begin to watch this film, ask them to turn the colours up brighter, bolder, stronger and turn the sounds up even louder.

7. Tell them to notice what they notice. Can they see themselves in this film? Are they walking around, talking to people? What is it that they can see? Tell them they don't need to answer you right now, just to pay attention and notice it.

8. Ask them to see what they *see, hear what they hear and notice* how good watching this movie makes them feel. This is that time in the future when everything is just going to go exactly as they'd like it to.

9. Allow them to really enjoy this moment and tell them that they can do whatever they feel they need to do to this image to make it even happier. They are the star of their very own cinema screening. As they see themselves in this movie, can they notice details about themselves? What are they wearing; how are they walking and moving around and what does the expression on their face look like? Ideally, they'll be seeing themselves looking really confident with a big, big smile on their face. And if they're not, then tell your child to do whatever they need to do right now to make this image ten times better. Enhancing the colours and the sounds will help to enhance the good feelings too.

10. After a few moments of enjoying this process, you can ask your child to open their eyes and discuss the events with you. Talking it through with you will help the ideas to crystallise in your child's mind.

Remember, this exercise is designed to help your child feel they can overcome any challenges they have in life at the moment, so they will want to see themselves reaching their goal.

SECTION FOUR

PUTTING IT INTO PRACTICE

In this section, I'll be showing you how I regularly use the techniques and strategies I've detailed in the previous sections, with some of the children who've visited me in my London clinic. Reading through these stories will help you to see how you can use them effectively too.

You'll notice that the same techniques pop up time and again – this is because the structure of a fear or phobia is pretty much the same every time, despite the fact that the details may change.

The good thing about this is that once you have an understanding of how anxiety is created by the mind and a knowledge of what to do about it, you'll be able to handle your child's concerns more easily.

Please do remember that these techniques, whilst very effective, should be regarded as 'first aid'. If your child continues to suffer with an anxiety related issue that proves to be difficult to resolve, then do please consult a practitioner who will be able to help you more.

9

General worries

It's easy to dismiss worries as simply a lightweight version of real anxiety and something that can be ignored. But the only difference between the two is that worries take place in the mind and anxiety is felt in the body. Both occur in response to future events whether real or imagined. Left unchecked, worries can and do create real feelings of anxiety, so it's good to nip them in the bud.

It doesn't help that we've become a 24-hour news society with an endless stream of information filtering into our homes whether we want it to or not, so if a random terrorist attack or disaster happens, it's not always easy to protect our children from hearing the gruesome details.

Attempting to come up with answers to questions and concerns about things that have never happened and are never likely to happen can wear you out and often embed the worries more deeply in your child's psyche. However, there are steps you can take that will make dealing with this much easier.

1. **Be prepared.** It's worth getting a 'story' clear in your mind in advance, working out what you'll say and how you're going to say it. When anxiety is created by a stressful news item on TV, it's not always easy to simply put on a brave face and reassure your child that there's 'nothing to worry about'. Ask other parents how they plan to explain the situation to their child – it may give you a few useful ideas.

2. **"Will this happen to me?"** is the first thought that will be running through your child's mind. They'll be wondering how this will impact on their own safety and whether this is going to

start happening in the street right outside their home. Reassure your child that this is happening 'far, far away'. Distance can be hard for children to imagine, so get a map or globe and point out that it's no where near their home or school.

3. **Give plenty of time.** Spend extra time sitting with your child, especially at bedtime, and listen carefully to their concerns. Every child is different and depending on their age and temperament will have a different perspective on the news stories. It's possible to worry your child even more by giving too much information in your conversations, so try to learn what 'specifically' it is that is worrying your child. It may not be as bad as you think and a simple answer may be all that's required.

4. **Empathise.** Use phrases such as: "*I can see that you're feeling worried / scared / anxious and that's understandable. It's a horrible thing that has happened.*"

5. **Avoid using negative phrases such as:**

   - *Don't worry.*
   - *Just stop thinking about it.*
   - *Don't keep going on about it or you'll make it worse.*
   - *Stop talking about it because you're starting to scare your little brother!* (Say this and don't be surprised if 'little brother' starts crying.)

   Remember, our mind makes pictures or images out of the words that we think or hear. Using a negative word will mean your child will end up doing exactly what you don't want them to do – worry!

6. **Reassure your child that we're safe.** Tell your child that when horrible things happen, there are lots of people who are looking after us and will keep us safe – e.g. Government, Police, teachers, mums and dads. They'll make sure that this doesn't happen to us and they also find the bad people and put them into prison.

Always use words that reflect the desired state, such as:

- *It's OK, we're all safe.*
- *We can stay calm about this, because it's happening far, far away.*
- *We can relax now, because there are plenty of people taking care of this for us.*
- *The situation is over now – it's finished.*

7. **Use the analogy of a false alarm to explain anxiety.** Liken your child's feelings of anxiety to a smoke alarm going off when it's got a bit too smoky in the kitchen from the cooking. The smoke alarm can't tell the difference between the house being on fire and a piece of toast getting overcooked under the grill – it will make the same amount of noise regardless – it's a 'false alarm'. And sometimes when our bodies feel a bit panicky and anxious, the same kind of thing is happening. Our bodies make a bit of a 'mistake' and worry us for no reason – there is no real danger.

While I've advocated that talking about problems is a good thing, sometimes words are best avoided. It's easy to tie yourself in knots trying to reassure your child and if it's not working, then *no* words are better than the *wrong* words – a hug or a cuddle might be better.

You'll desperately be trying to formulate answers and reassurances for things that may or may not happen and your child will resolutely keep on going round and round in circles, talking about their fears and concerns.

"Yes, but what happens if I get there and there's no-one to play with?"

or

"What if I have no-one to sit next to?"

These are common worries about the future but none of us has a crystal ball. You don't know what might happen and if you pretend you do, you could actually make things worse.

You can initially empathise with your child by saying something like:

"Oh yes, I can understand how that makes you feel. You felt a little like that when you went to James's party didn't you? And then you easily found a few friends to play with."

Acknowledging the worry is often all that's needed to make it go away. And then I recommend parking the conversation by following this exercise.

Exercise: The Worry Box

1. Find a box. It can be an old shoebox, or a small, attractively decorated one so long as it has a lid and can be closed easily. Include your child in this selection and tell them it can be any sort of box that feels right for them. Explain to your child that this is going to be their personal Worry Box.

2. Put a supply of paper and coloured felt-tip pens inside the box. Each time your child gets stuck in a cycle of worries, ask them to have a think about what might be making them feel like this.

3. Take one of the sheets of paper from the Worry Box and ask your child to choose a coloured pen. Having a good selection of coloured pens is useful because you can ask your child what colour they think this worry is.

4. Ask them to write down the worry, or draw a picture that represents it.

5. Once they've finished, ask them to fold the piece of paper and put it into the Worry Box. Put the lid firmly on the box and put it away.

(Hint: It's best to keep this box somewhere out of everyday sight, e.g. the top of a cupboard. Don't store it in the bedroom and certainly not under the bed, otherwise your child will be sleeping 'on their worries' and that's not a good idea.)

6. By writing the worry down, they will have sent an important message to the subconscious mind, letting it know that the emotional message has been received loud and clear and that it's been acted upon.

7. Each time another worry begins to aggravate your child, follow the same process. Ask them to write it down, fold up the paper and pop it into the box.

8. Over a surprisingly short space of time, you'll find the worries begin to evaporate and will cease to keep nagging your child.

9. At the end of each week, sit down with your child, open the box and empty out the pieces of paper. Read through the worries together and encourage your child to be as pleasantly surprised as you when you both discover that most of them took care of themselves, without requiring any action from either of you whatsoever.

Remember – most of the things that we worry about never happen!

DEVELOPING RESILIENCE

In today's society there are more and more ways in which we hold a 'mirror' up to our children, pointing out their shortcomings and inadequacies. Thanks to the new 'selfie culture' it's not easy to hide that zit on the end of your nose, or your lank, greasy hair. And it's the same at school. Perpetual SATS tests and examinations mean that today's children are 'weighed, measured and tested' more than any other generation and from a far earlier age too. No wonder it results in anxious, worried children who lack the confidence to step outside into the big, wide world.

It's often been said that life is a contact sport, so it's inevitable that sooner or later we're going to get hurt. Boosting your child's 'resilience' is what will inoculate them against life's knocks and setbacks. It gives them the ability to pick themselves up, dust themselves down and carry on.

Resilient children:

- have the ability to bounce back from negative situations;
- tend to be more optimistic in their outlook;
- can think creatively when faced with difficulties;
- are socially competent with close friendships;
- are able to communicate well.

Resilience is a skill that anyone can learn and given that your child is unlikely to pass every exam they sit, sail through every job interview they attend and find that the path of true love runs smoothly, it's a valuable resource to have.

As a key member of your child's 'support team' you can:

1. Help them to see negative events as part and parcel of day-to-day life. It's not an automatic disaster if something goes wrong; it just means that a different solution needs to be found. Talk openly about mistakes that you may have made yourself and laugh about them: *"Silly me, I put my car keys in the fridge!" "That recipe didn't work well did it? I thought it tasted odd. Next time, I'll try it without the tomatoes and I'll add carrots instead."* Don't pretend everything is always perfect.

2. If your child seems to be repeatedly failing, check that they're not setting unrealistic goals for themselves. Help your child to break goals down into smaller steps, so that they become more manageable.

3. Teach your child to problem-solve by bouncing ideas around at one of your 'family chats'. Not every idea that gets mentioned will be a good one, but this is a natural part of the process. Write them down and tell your child that the aim is to come up with ten different solutions to each problem, however wacky they may seem, and then you can reject the ones you decide not to use.

4. Get more involved with school life, whether it's as a parent doing things like baking cakes for the school fete or building scenery for the end of term play, or encouraging your child to join the choir or sports team. Attending all the events that happen out of school hours as a family will help your child feel that this is somewhere that he or she truly belongs.

5. Most importantly, model the behaviour you wish to see. Demonstrate good communication skills in your own relationships and start incorporating these 'bounce-back' skills in your own attitude to daily life.

DEALING WITH NEGATIVE THINKING

Negative thinking is a bad habit that many children (and adults for that matter) slip into. Left unchecked, it begins to eat away at confidence levels, so watch out for the language that your child is using and reframe their sentences with a positive spin.

For example, if your child says:

"There won't be anyone at my new school who likes me."

It may seem tempting to reply with:

"Don't be so daft, of course there will."

It's better to give a fuller, more considered answer with a positive outlook:

"I completely understand why you're worried that you won't make any new friends, but the advantage of going to a bigger school is that there will be many more children to choose from than there ever were at your junior school. So, the chances of meeting new friends you will get along with are actually very high. Yes, I dare say you'll come across one or two children who you won't like and likewise, perhaps they won't be keen on being friendly with you either, but you can simply see that as an opportunity to move on and get to know other new people."

OR

"Do we have to go to Grandma's house? It's so boring there!"

Rather than replying:

"Yes you do. Stop moaning because you'll be fine when you get there."

It would be better to reframe your answer as:

"I know it's not the same as being at home with your computer games, nor will you have your friends there, but remember how much you enjoyed going last time. When you walked her dog Rolo down by the riverbank, he jumped in and chased those swans and made us all laugh. I wonder what he'll get up to this time."

Negative thinking, along with whingeing, whining and moaning, can easily become a habit that's hard to break. Switching your child's thought patterns around will help to prevent this from happening. And don't forget to keep a check on yourself too. Is your own negative outlook fuelling your child's negativity perhaps?

POSITIVE THINKING

Exercise

1. Encourage your child to start keeping a journal or diary. They can use a physical notebook to record events or doodle in, or they can use their smartphones or tablet device for the same purpose. They can call their journal anything they like: Happiness Diary, Sunshine book . . . etc.

2. Ask your child to write down three positive things that happened in their day. These can be quite simple things to begin with, e.g. We had pizza for lunch and it's my favourite; the maths teacher forgot to set homework for us; it was a sunny day today and we played outside.

Repeat this on a daily basis. If your child is reluctant to physically sit down and do this on a daily basis, introduce this technique conversationally, either in the car on the way home from school, or as you're sitting round the dinner table, or in the evenings at bath-time. You can start the ball rolling by mentioning something really good that happened to yourself during the day – and then taking turns.

If your child really cannot come up with three positive things that happened in their day, then my recommendation is to increase the required number to five or even ten things. Strange as it may seem, this will help to free up your child's mind and they'll start to notice smaller, less significant occurrences, e.g. A butterfly flew into the room; I watched one of my favourite TV programmes.

Bear in mind, it's the flow of the thought patterns that's the important bit and not the events themselves. Once you've got this going in the right direction, you'll quickly see how it becomes a natural part of your child's thinking.

10

Stage fright, auditions, interviews

Does your child sing and perform like a little superstar in the privacy of the bathroom, only to shrivel with embarrassment when performing in front of others?

We all want confident children don't we, but it might help initially to think about what confidence is – how does it differ from self-esteem and how do we know when we've got it?

We've all seen children who strut around the playground constantly bragging and boasting. A bit too boisterous and loud, they're invariably pushing to be first in the queue. Few of us would want our children to behave like that because it's pretty obvious that overly confident 'outside' behaviour doesn't really match a person's 'inside' feelings. It's simply there to mask feelings of insecurity and they're not genuinely confident children.

Confidence is having the belief that you can succeed at something. It's possible to be confident about one area of your life but totally unconfident about another. You might feel confident about your cooking skills, for example, but feel completely out of your depth when it comes to filling in tax returns.

Your self-esteem, on the other hand, is related to a broad sense of personal value or self-worth. It's not a quality that changes very much as it's more about how you see yourself as a person in general rather than your ability to specifically do something. Discussing your family's values (with regards to honesty, trust, work, spirituality, etc.) will encourage this part of your child's identity to develop more easily. They'll get a sense of who and what they are from your family's 'brand'.

Building confidence comes from taking action and trying out things that are difficult – stepping out of the comfort zone. It's not about being perfect, it's about facing obstacles and realising that it's OK to fail – you can always have another go.

In the early years, confidence develops from becoming successful at doing things independently round the home – the more opportunities you can put in your child's path, the better. Patience from you will also play a part. If you cannot wait patiently for your child to do up their shoelaces, climb a flight of stairs or cut up their own food, you'll be denting their confidence. Taking over to speed things up or showing signs of frustration will not foster feelings of success.

Likewise telling your child that they're not reciting their poem well enough and should put more effort into it will not enable them to stand on stage and give an Oscar-winning performance. Using negative phrases such as *"Don't speak so quietly – no-one will hear you"* will ensure that you get just that: a quiet child that no-one can hear.

HANNAH – AGE 14

Hannah had been offered the lead part in her school play and was in two minds about accepting it. It would be fair to say that she was not an obvious choice for a starring role as she didn't have a naturally outgoing personality. However, this year's play was a musical and Hannah was known for her singing ability and she loved doing it. Singing alongside a teacher in her music lessons though was very different to performing on stage. She'd had few opportunities for doing this and it was one of the reasons why her teachers had offered her the main part in the play.

Hannah was nervous and one of her biggest worries was that she'd start blushing as soon as she walked on stage. She felt cross and frustrated with herself. She told me she often practised singing in front of her bedroom mirror at home and knew she could put on an amazing performance, so why was it that as soon as she tried to do it in front of an audience, she felt herself becoming small?

I explained that this was a natural reaction – human beings have a built-in need to be accepted by their peers because our survival depends on being part of a group. Putting ourselves forward in order to be judged means we potentially jeopardise this – hence the feelings of anxiety.

These are the steps I took to help Hannah:

STEP 1: TFT – TAPPING TECHNIQUE

As you'll see I often use this Tapping therapy (p. 77) before carrying out any other exercises. I find it really helps to take the 'heat' out of a situation and I felt it to be even more appropriate to use with Hannah as she mentioned her fear of blushing.

STEP 2: STOP BLUSHING NOW

We've all experienced those moments of self-consciousness that irritatingly trigger off a reddening of the skin – most usually on the face. Blushing from embarrassment is connected to your 'fight-or-flight' response. When you find yourself in an awkward situation, your body automatically releases a rush of adrenaline that then causes your breathing and heart rate to speed up, enabling you to run away from this perceived danger, if you need to.

Adrenaline also causes your blood vessels to dilate in order to improve blood flow and oxygen delivery and this is the case with blushing. The veins in your face dilate and as more blood flows through them, your face becomes red.

I asked Hannah to think back to the last time she blushed. Could she remember what was going through her mind? Very often people are thinking something along the lines of: *"Oh no, I think I'm going to go red. Yes, I am, I just know it – I'm turning red. I hope they don't notice my face going red. I can feel it – it's starting to turn red. Great, last thing I wanted – my face going red!"*

She agreed and realised exactly why her face did turn red. Her internal dialogue issued a command, her mind created a picture and her body followed – doing exactly as she had told it to.

I explained that she could easily take control of this by giving a different sort of command. The next time she felt herself starting to get that rush of adrenaline that signalled that her face might start turning red, all she simply needed to say was:

"I think I'm turning BLUE – yes, I am – I'm turning BLUE. I can feel that BLUENESS starting to spread across my face, my chest and down my arms even – I'm turning BLUE."

As it's usual to feel heat rising up our faces, instruct this feeling to travel in a downwards direction, like so:

"I can feel the BLUE start to drain down from the top of my head, down through my face, my eyes, my cheeks . . . down my neck, my shoulders, my chest. Yes, I'm definitely turning BLUE."

And you can also add other suggestions such as a bucket of ice being tipped over the head or just a couple of ice cubes sitting on top of the head.

You can test this out – it works!

STEP 3: REFRAME

I also pointed out that feelings of nervousness and those of excitement are really very similar and told Hannah to make sure she wasn't confusing the two. It's common to hear top performers describe their feelings of a tightness in the stomach, sweaty palms and a racing heartbeat as an indication that they're pumped up and ready to go on stage – they know they're feeling excited! And those feelings are very similar to anxiety.

It was time to reframe her feelings and I encouraged her to change her internal dialogue for the words: *"I feel excited and I'm looking forward to singing"* each time she felt those 'butterflies in her tummy'.

STEP 4: SPIN THOSE FEELINGS AWAY

The next step to tackling the wobbly feelings in her tummy was to use the spinning exercise (p. 97). Hannah was able to change the direction the feelings were travelling in and also made sure that they were spinning ten times faster than before to heighten that sense of feeling good.

STEP 5: CONFIDENCE ANCHOR

It's important to always remember to put a set of extra good feelings in after having worked on removing unwanted anxious feelings, otherwise your body will feel as if there is an 'empty space'. Leave this vacant and your mind will very quickly find something to put back in there. That 'something' will often be the exact same unpleasant feelings you've just spent time removing, for it will feel like the most natural thing to do.

I worked on creating a confidence anchor (p. 104) for Hannah. I asked her to come up with three occasions from the past when she had felt really confident and had sung her very best.

She was able to come up with two occasions – the first was when she'd had the opportunity to record a few songs at a recording studio, which was a visit her parents had arranged for her. The second was when she sang solo in the church choir.

She felt a bit stuck when trying to come up with another occasion when she had felt truly confident singing her heart out. I remembered her telling me that she often sang in front of her bedroom mirror and loved belting out the songs and feeling like a true professional, so we used this scenario too.

I 'anchored' the three memories for her and showed her how she would be able to use her confidence anchor during her performances in the school play. Fortunately, Hannah had a six-week run of rehearsals before opening night and this gave her the time to test out the work we had done together. As I expected, her performance in the play was a success and when I spoke to her mother a few weeks later she told me Hannah was continuing to use the techniques on a regular basis and they could see the difference it was making to her overall feelings of self-belief.

11

Phobia

Fear of dogs

In this section, I'm going to focus on Imani who came to see me with a phobia of dogs, but the same protocol can be followed to tackle other phobias that may have developed as a result of a nasty experience.

A survey carried out by the Dogs Trust in 2016 showed that 37% of 2000 parents said their children were fearful of dogs. And 25% of these said it affects their child's daily life. One in seven parents admitted to also being scared, often as a result of a bad experience from childhood.

I have a lot of sympathy with these figures for I too had an intense fear of dogs from the age of 5 and can easily remember the feelings of dread that would spread through my body if a dog came anywhere near me. I didn't truly get over this fear until I became a dog owner myself and now when I take him out for walks, I can still feel a slight sense of uneasiness if I spot a dog that I think might cause trouble. I view this as a good thing – having the ability to anticipate a problem is what keeps us human beings safe and well and I would never want to get to the stage where I couldn't have those feelings. The only difference in me now is that I feel I could confidently tackle a problem situation should one ever arise – and that's how it should be.

Intense fears and phobias usually begin with coming into contact with something – in this case, the scary dog. Or it will come about from hearing about someone else's horrible experience or witnessing it, either in real life or on the TV. Remember, the mind can't tell the difference between reality and a made-up scary movie.

The fight or flight response will kick in – palpitations, shortness of breath, sick tummy, legs and feet that feel like they're made of concrete – it will feel horrible – and then we'll learn that we have to avoid that situation in order not to feel like that again. Of course, what we're trying to avoid is the uncomfortable feeling – and not the dog. But the two become inextricably linked and so avoiding the dog seems the most sensible thing to do.

As I explained in Chapter 2, one of the clever things our brain does is make 'generalisations'. It stops us from having to relearn how to open a door each time we encounter a new one. Once we've experienced opening a small variety of doors, we feel confident that we could figure out pretty much how to open every door we meet from now on. That's the good part.

The downside is that we only need to encounter one unfriendly, nasty dog to immediately make the sweeping generalisation that all dogs, regardless of size, colour and breed, are dangerous and should be avoided at all costs.

Parents will often opt for the 'avoidance strategy' through exhaustion or a lack of options – it seems like the most sensible thing to do at the time. In the short-term this works but in the long-term it will make the problem worse. Here I will give you some other options.

IMANI – AGE 8

Imani developed a severe phobia of dogs after being chased by a large, bouncy Dalmatian while walking through the woods with her parents. Not only was she taken aback by the dog's over-enthusiasm, when she started to scream for it to go away, it started to bark at her. The more she shrieked, the louder the dog got. To Imani, the dog seemed huge – she felt as if he were almost as tall as her. Doubly upsetting was the fact that her favourite film was *101 Dalmatians* so in her mind, all Dalmatians were cute puppies and so she was shocked that this could be happening to her. Her trust in dogs was completely shattered.

STEP 1: GRADUAL DESENSITISATION

It's natural to see things in black or white – I will either be afraid of dogs, or I won't. And trying to imagine yourself not being scared is sometimes too big a leap for us to make, so the mind will automatically drag you back to feeling scared. After all, feeling scared will be a familiar state for the body to be in and although it's unpleasant, it can feel safer than imagining yourself as someone who is confident in the company of dogs.

I suggested some initial first steps that Imani's parents could take:

1. To acknowledge Imani's fears and have a conversation about how she was feeling – remember, putting words to feelings can help take the sting out of a bad situation.

2. To keep reminding her that not all dogs are unpleasant and need to be feared. It's just that one particular dog that got over-excited.

3. To create a 'vision board' that can hang on her bedroom wall. Look for pictures of friendly looking dogs either in magazines or print off from the internet. Stick them on the board and look at them regularly. Point out that dogs come in all sorts of shapes and sizes and have different temperaments. Keep emphasising this – not all dogs are the same – just like your friends at school – some are your favourite friends and others are not.

4. Read story books and watch films that have great dogs as a main character.

5. Buy a dog cuddly toy. Or a t-shirt with a dog motif.

6. Portray dogs in a good light by searching on the internet for dogs that help people – for example, guide dogs for the blind and hearing dogs for the deaf, sniffer dogs that rescue people in avalanches, working dogs that round up sheep, etc.

7. Visit the local park and sit on a bench and watch dogs from a distance.

8. Buddy up with a friend who has a reliably well-behaved dog and go for a walk together.

9. Learn how to touch and stroke a friendly dog.

This is just an example of how a gradual desensitisation approach could work – you may be able to think of other more suitable steps to put in there. There will be a temptation to hurry these steps along, but taking your time over each one before moving on to the next is more likely to produce a successful outcome.

STEP 2: DEALING WITH NEGATIVE THINKING

I asked Imani's parents to help her think of other times when she felt nervous but became brave, e.g. jumping into the swimming pool; riding a bicycle without stabilisers; going to a friend's party; speaking out loud in front of the class or taking part in the school play. It's important to build up the idea that despite feeling like a scaredy-cat, she has proved that she has faced challenges before and dealt with them successfully.

STEP 3: TFT TAPPING TECHNIQUE

Imani continued to experience feelings of anxiety each time she remembered the episode in the woods with the dog. I showed her how to use the Tapping technique (p. 77) and advised her parents to use it with her each evening and morning for at least a week. This will help to reduce the build-up of anxiety that had occurred during the few weeks since the unhappy episode.

STEP 4: CHANGING SCARY PICTURES

Imani continued to experience unpleasant images in her mind, especially at night-time when she struggled to fall asleep. She could see the dog in the woods clearly – she could see his teeth and hear his barking. The more she tried to forget about him, the harder it became.

I showed her how to use the Magic TV Control (p. 86) to change those pictures and sounds. I asked her to shrink that image of the dog right down till it was just a tiny little thing no higher than her ankle. I then asked her to switch that TV channel to one that was showing cute dogs only – she was able to choose her favourite ones from her vision board.

TWO WEEKS LATER . . .

Imani returned feeling much calmer. I repeated the Tapping technique and checked that she was able to use the TV Control technique effectively.

STEP 5: CONFIDENCE ANCHOR

At some point, we would be asking Imani to return to the woods for a walk with her parents. I wanted to give her something she could take with her to help her feel brave and set up a confidence anchor (p. 104) for her.

STEP 6: YOUR BRIGHT, NEW, SHINY FUTURE

We finished off with a guided visualisation that enabled her to mentally rehearse the future walk in the woods (p. 110). Rehearsing difficult situations in your imagination before having to go through them for real is a clever way of allowing your body to feel as if it has already experienced it. When you go to do it for real, you'll feel more relaxed about it, believing that this is something you've done successfully many times before.

***

This whole process took one month from start to finish – I know most of us would like to solve problems quicker but taking slower steps means results are more likely to become deeply embedded and remain for life.

12

Fear of spiders and snakes

Many of us develop a fear of spiders and snakes but it's never been clear whether we're born with this fear or develop it over time. A venomous bite from one of these creatures lurking in the grass would have proved fatal for our ancestors so it is possible that over time this strong desire to avoid them has become deeply embedded in our subconscious minds.

A study published in 2008 in *Cognition* and another in 2014 in the journal *Evolution & Human Behaviour* both point to an inherited fear of spiders and snakes. It is, however, possible to delete this strong phobic reaction.

I assisted Paul McKenna on many of his seminars designed to cure phobias – he would spend the morning and early afternoon reframing delegates' fears and then use a mixture of NLP techniques and hypnosis to get everyone feeling calm and relaxed. Later in the afternoon, experienced keepers would bring in tarantulas and pythons from the local zoo. It was astonishing to see just how many people who'd arrived in the morning shaking at the mention of the word 'snake,' would then be capable of not only stroking a snake but also in many cases being able to pick one up, wrapping it around their neck.

Not too many of us have encountered a live snake so dealing with this particular phobia is similar to dealing with 'a scary monster under the bed'. It doesn't exist and it's more the idea or thought of it that will bring on the phobic reaction – although seeing a picture or a movie that has a snake in it can make a person feel really uncomfortable.

A spider phobia, on the other hand, is often accompanied by memories of an actual encounter and so there are often two aspects to the problem to deal with.

CAMERON – AGE 14

Cameron came to visit me for help with his spider phobia. His father came along to the session with him and told me that he had come along because he too suffered from a dreadful spider phobia. He'd lived in Australia as a child and had never got over the size of the spiders there, nor how he felt. We agreed that it was understandable that he felt this way, for he was always being warned by adults to 'watch out for the spiders' and this sense of vigilance had never left him. He told me that now at the age of 50, he could still shake and scream at the sight of an ordinary house spider and felt quite ridiculous at doing so, but had accepted that he would 'never be cured'. He was aware that he'd passed his fear onto Cameron, who was struggling now to go into their sitting room at home because he'd seen a large spider there a few months ago, and was seeking help for him because he didn't want him to suffer in the way that he had all his life.

Of course, to begin with I winced when I heard Cameron's father say he would 'never be cured', because this is a lovely hypnotic suggestion to give his son. How could Cameron ever believe that he could feel fine in the company of spiders when his father was telling him it just was not possible?

I started to ask Cameron how the problem had started and discovered that he'd always been mildly scared of spiders but he'd been able to avoid them and his mum usually got rid of any that were round the house. But a few months ago, his parents went out for the evening and he and his younger sister were left with the family au pair – a 19-year-old French girl. As they sat in the sitting room watching TV that evening, a large spider ran across the room and the au pair had started to scream and scream. She ran out of the room and was too scared to go back in. Cameron and his sister ran out with her and the three of them sat together in the kitchen for the rest of the evening until the parents returned home.

In this case, the spider was never found and so understandably, Cameron had been left with the worry that it was still there somewhere, lurking under the sofa waiting to pounce. It's worth reminding ourselves that spiders are more scared of us than we are of them, so they'll usually run and hide themselves in nooks and crannies and not come out again.

But Cameron also now had a secondary fear – that of being left alone in the care of their au pair. Not only was he nervous about his parents going out, leaving him and his sister, but he also felt panicky if ever they had to go out with the au-pair, and actually very cross with her.

I worked with Cameron in the usual way: breaking down the problem into smaller individual ones.

STEP 1: TFT TAPPING THERAPY

I knew from the story Cameron had told me that the event in the sitting room that fateful evening had shaken him up significantly and we would have to work on more than just his fear of spiders. I used the Tapping technique (p. 77) to reduce his anxiety levels so we would be able to do further work with visualisation.

STEP 2: CHANGING PICTURES

When I asked Cameron to describe the image he could see in his mind each time I mentioned the word 'spider', he described an enormous tarantula that didn't resemble the ordinary small house spider they'd had in the sitting room in the slightest. It was probably more like Dad's description of nasty spiders in Australia. I changed this image for Cameron using the Magic TV Control technique (p. 86). We played around with it; made it look comical by dressing it up in a football hat and scarf and gave it a squeaky Mickey Mouse type voice. Cameron laughed at this so I knew he was able to see this new, funny image clearly. And then I asked him to use his TV Control to switch the picture off and send it away completely.

Something interesting to note: As Cameron and I were talking, the room became warmer and Dad hadn't taken off his coat and before long (because I have quite a hypnotic voice) he fell asleep. To begin with this wasn't a problem, but after a few minutes Dad began to snore. Cameron was terribly embarrassed by this but I told him not to worry – I was used to this and took it as a compliment if someone fell asleep when I was talking.

STEP 3: HYPNOSIS

I finished our first session with some hypnosis – a guided visualisation where I had Cameron see himself walking back into the sitting room (something he had not been able to do since 'that' evening). I asked him to see himself feeling comfortable, calm and relaxed sitting on the sofa and as he did so, I gave him plenty of positive suggestions that all his spider worries were gradually evaporating.

And then just as the session was ending, Dad woke up – and off they went.

TWO WEEKS LATER . . .

Cameron was feeling a bit more relaxed but hadn't got rid of his fear completely. Dad, on the other hand, told me he felt completely cured! Never in his wildest dreams did he believe that he would get rid of his fear and yet somehow he had. To be honest, never in *my* wildest dreams did I imagine that something like this would happen!

Although he had fallen asleep, his subconscious mind had absorbed all the positive messages I'd given Cameron and now he felt calm and relaxed whenever he thought about spiders. Sounds a bit too good to be true, doesn't it? But Cameron's Dad did contact me six months later and happily told me that he still felt completely over his life-long spider phobia.

Cameron felt disheartened that he hadn't had such a quick response, but I was not surprised. I explained that for him, the embarrassment of having his father asleep in the corner of the room meant his brain was flooded with stress chemicals and this would have diverted his attention away from the work we were doing.

I could also see that Cameron's feelings of anxiety were wrapped up in his feelings of being let down by the au pair – she was supposed to have protected him and his sister and taken control of the situation, but she'd let them down.

STEP 4: HAVENING TECHNIQUES

I felt the Havening Techniques therapy (p. 83) would be ideal for dealing with Cameron's feelings of nervousness. I taught him how to use this means of self-soothing and it was something he did every evening. He'd told me that he felt at his most vulnerable in the evenings for that was the time of day that the original event had happened.

It took a couple more sessions for Cameron to start seeing and feeling the same benefits as those his father was enjoying.

13

Medical anxiety

Doctors, injections and germs

No-one enjoys medical appointments but it's important to remind yourself that your child will be looking to you as the authority figure in these situations and the slightest hint of anxiety from you will have a significant impact on how they feel too. The more confident an air you can give off, the better for them.

Avoid talking about the doctor or dentist's surgery in a negative way – even grumbling about the length of time you've had to wait for an appointment, the grubby carpet or the miserable receptionist will start to sow seeds of doubt in your child's mind. Thinking that going to the doctors is going to be an unpleasant experience leads to feelings of powerlessness and pain – and that is precisely what will be experienced. Having a more positive mindset and thinking that going to the doctors will help you to feel better – or stay healthy – will change the outcome. Not only will your child feel happier but they genuinely will get better quicker too as the *placebo effect* will kick in.

WORDS THAT WORK

As I've pointed out many times, the words that get spoken to and heard by your child will have an impact on how they feel and cope with situations. I do so hate hearing medics use the words 'sharp scratch' – of course I understand the need for staff to warn the recipient of an upcoming injection in case it startles them and they snatch their arm away, but I would prefer them to say something more positive such as 'special medicine coming in now'.

It's worth remembering this when thinking about what you'll be saying to your child. Here are a couple of responses I came up with to the question *"Will it hurt?"*:

- *"Well, I imagine you will feel a little something but it will be over quickly. Remember how last week, you fell off the slide and hurt your knee? That was a big bump and hurt quite a bit, but this will be very, very small."*

- *"As you press the cotton wool against the side of your arm, you'll notice that the sting is starting to stop. A couple of seconds and it will be gone. You're feeling good now – proud of yourself."*

INFORMATION

The more your child knows about what to expect, the easier it will be for them to deal with the procedure. Here are a few things you can do in advance to get your child used to the idea of having a medical appointment:

- Read a few of the many story books available that give details of medical visits.

- Practise an upcoming procedure on dolls and teddies.

- Shine torches into each other's mouths and look in mirrors.

- Recount stories from your own childhood. Children love hearing stories about the time that Grandma took Mum or Dad for a similar appointment.

Start desensitising your child in advance. Arrange frequent visits to the doctor or dentist, for reasons not associated with illnesses or injections. These could be to collect prescriptions, make appointments or just to pick up a leaflet. Ideally your child's first trip to the dentist should be accompanying you on a dental exam – this will normalise the situation.

- Make sure appointment times for visits and procedures are clearly marked in the diary so your child has time to prepare. Springing it on them as a surprise on the actual day will be met with resistance, whereas a pre-scheduled activity is easier to cope with.

DISTRACTION TECHNIQUES

It can be helpful to think about what to do to distract your child during an unpleasant procedure and here are some examples:

- Hold a cuddly toy on a lap and ask the nurse or doctor to 'do' teddy first.

- Learn the Tapping technique and use it during the procedure.

- Blow out imaginary birthday candles or take some bubble mixture with you and ask your child to blow through the wand.

- Hold a mobile phone in the other hand and have the stopwatch running as you child counts the number of seconds it takes for the procedure.

- Future pace – start talking about what you'll be doing *after* the event – going to the shops, stopping off at a friend's house, how good it will be to go back home and tell everyone about your visit.

FEAR OF GERMS

This is a common worry for children and it's not all that surprising given that we live in a world where they constantly hear the following references:

- TV adverts promote products that promise to kill 99% of all germs.

- We're encouraged to use anti-bacterial handwashes and even carry anti-bacterial gels in our handbags – *just in case*.

- Children are given vaccinations – to stop germs and illnesses.

- They're often told not to come to school if they're ill to 'stop germs spreading'.

- When we're ill we avoid seeing friends in case we give them our germs or worse still, they give us theirs.

Avoiding germs can become an obsession for some children. I worked with one little girl who refused to go anywhere near her brother long after he'd recovered from a nasty cold. She would scream out loud if she came into close contact with him. Her mother told me it was making family life difficult as she wouldn't sit in the back of the car with him, nor on the same sofa when watching TV, even if they were at opposite ends.

REFRAMING

- Gradually start reframing the concept of germs in your conversations. There are thousands of different species of germs – good and friendly bacteria as well as bad bacteria.

- Most germs are good for us because having a supply of bacteria living inside us means they'll help fight off the really bad bacteria if they try to visit us.

- We have so many germs and bacteria living on and inside of us that it would be impossible to get rid of them all. Doctors are now discovering that many health problems are caused by a lack of germs and not because of them.

- Children who live on farms get exposed to far more germs than those who live in cities – and they tend to be healthier.

- Healthy diets which include eating lots of vegetables, help to fight off bad germs.

VIJAY – AGE 8

Vijay's mother brought him to see me as he had a real fear of doctors and in particular needles. He'd had his last round of vaccinations at age 4 and his mother said she didn't think he could remember this occasion, but he had been present when his younger sister had hers, just a year ago. She had cried considerably and this had upset Vijay.

Vijay had been ill recently with a virus and wasn't recovering as quickly as he should have been. The doctors had suggested a blood test for him to rule out more serious reasons for his lack of energy. Each time his mother brought up the subject with him, Vijay had thrown a bit of a tantrum. She was concerned it was going to be a struggle to get him into the doctors' surgery for the test.

STEP 1: HAVENING TECHNIQUES

I felt the first step in helping Vijay feel calmer was to run through the Havening Techniques (p. 83). I combined this with talking about his sister's vaccinations and managed to reframe this nasty experience into a positive one that will help her stay safe and healthy in the future.

I also wanted to teach Vijay's mother the Havening treatment. I asked her to run through the soothing routines at home each day as this would begin to remove the anxiety from her son's body. I also recommended that she use it on herself as it would help if she too could feel calmer.

I also told her that I would want her to use it in the room when Vijay goes for his blood test. I recommended that she sit opposite him so he can see her while she Havens herself. This will fire off what's known as 'mirror neurons' inside Vijay's mind – the simple act of watching his mother run through this procedure will trigger off the same soothing benefits that he would experience if it were being done to him. This was another reason for them to practise the procedure at home on a regular basis – so that his body could begin to build up an automatic response and begin to feel calm more promptly.

STEP 2: BREATHING TECHNIQUES

I also taught Vijay a breathing technique as this would not only act as a valuable distraction technique but also help to expel stress chemicals from the body. See p. 65 for ideas of how you can be creative with breathing. We agreed that Vijay would pretend to be blowing candles out on a birthday cake as he was having his blood taken. We weren't too sure how many he would have to blow out because we didn't know how long the procedure would take. I estimated 15 candles and he guessed a figure of 20. We agreed he'd let me know afterwards which one of us had 'won'.

STEP 3: GUIDED VISUALISATION

Finally, I did an eyes-closed routine and had Vijay 'see' himself going through the procedure. I knew he would be having an after-school appointment, so I started the visualisation at the point where his mum would be picking him up from school. I told the story of the journey to the doctor's surgery and filled in all the relevant details. I got him to see himself sitting in the chair having his blood taken as he blew out those imaginary birthday candles one by one. I told him he could also see his mother running through the Havening Techniques out of the corner of his eye, which was making him feel more and more comfortable by the minute.

This simple procedure is a clever way of helping your body feel as if it's experienced something many times before. Then when you turn up for the actual event, you automatically feel more relaxed as you know exactly what to expect.

I wrote a script for this guided visualisation and gave a print-out to his mother so she could read it to Vijay as a bedtime story each evening for a few days before his test.

TWO WEEKS LATER . . .

Vijay's mother called me to say things had gone well – even better, his blood test results had come back normal and Vijay had started to regain his energy. And as for the number of candles on that imaginary birthday cake – there were 17. So it was a very close result and we agreed that he was the winner – in more ways than one.

14

School refusal

School refusal – often accompanied by tantrums, meltdowns and running off in the opposite direction – can impact the whole family and prove embarrassing for siblings if the refusal takes place on school premises.

Quite often it may seem as if the refusal crops up out of nowhere and even overnight, whereas in fact, it's more likely to have been festering for some time and feelings of anxiety have simply built up until the child can no longer cope.

School refusal can range from separation anxiety that results in a few days missed here and there due to vague tummy aches, to those who miss weeks and even months at a time.

There's nothing worse for a parent than having to prise a clingy, distressed child off their body. It's natural to want to do everything you possibly can to comfort and soothe your child and yet, giving lots of hugs and cuddles can make the anxiety worse in the long run as it can reinforce the idea that being apart is painful or dangerous in some way.

Unless there is a real reason for your child to be fearful of attending school – such as ridicule or teasing by peers, an overly strict teacher, struggles with school work or bullying – then the problem usually stems from your child overestimating the risk of being separated from you and underestimating their abilities to cope with being apart. It's often hard for a child to describe their feelings of being unsafe and so it's not uncommon for them to describe it as a tummy ache or headache. Alternatively, feelings of anger which are fuelled by anxiety can result in tantrums, screaming and lashing out.

Remember that tackling school refusal is often a team effort – talk to the school, who should be used to managing this type of behaviour, and ask them for suggestions. Discuss any possible causes for the anxiety.

LIAM – AGE 9

When Liam and his mother came to see me, he hadn't been able to go to school for 4 months. There was no discernible reason for his refusal and his mother had had many conversations with the school about this. Fortunately, one of the teachers had now started to visit them at home once a week to set school work and encourage Liam to start thinking about returning. Liam had developed a good relationship with this particular teacher and wanted to return but couldn't get rid of his feelings of anxiety. He told me that each time he thought about going to school he felt as if there were *"black, wriggly worms"* in his tummy.

STEP 1: GAINING PERSPECTIVE

I started by helping Liam see that his mind had simply got into the habit of playing tricks on him, making him imagine that great dangers were lurking at school, rather than seeing the nice teacher and his friends – most of whom he was missing.

I taught him about the 'smoke alarm analogy' (p. 117 in Chapter 9) – the alarm will respond in exactly the same way regardless of whether there's a small piece of toast under the grill that's starting to blacken or a huge fire engulfing the whole house. Liam's inner 'alarm' was sending signals of danger when there really wasn't a need for them. It's simply making a mistake.

STEP 2: BREATHING EXERCISES

I taught Liam some breathing exercises – I explained that the most important thing was to remember to 'blow out' rather than take a deep breath in. I got him to look out of the window and focus on a tall building he could see in the far distance. There was a flag waving from the top of this building and I asked him to blow out slowly until he felt that his out breath had reached the flag. He kept blowing out for around 10 seconds.

I told him that he could do this in the morning on his way to school or he could curl up his hand in front of his mouth and imagine that it's a paper bag and blow into it five times slowly – long, slow puffs are what's needed.

Practising breathing exercises on a regular basis is what I recommend, as in an 'emergency' situation this will be your first port of call to calm your child down (p. 65).

STEP 3: TFT TAPPING

I taught Liam the Tapping technique (p. 77) and how to use the measurement scale (p. 54) so he could see how his anxiety reduced from level 8 down to level 1. It doesn't have to disappear completely and become a zero – so long as it's reduced, then we know that it is heading in the right direction.

STEP 4: WORDS THAT WORK

I showed Liam's mum how altering the words that she used when talking about the problem would also help to change his mindset. She started 'future-pacing' – using sentences such as *"When you go back to school"* and *"Pretty soon, you'll be able to go back to school easily . . . it's just one more of those things that you'll learn how to do."*

I also told her to use this phrase whenever Liam started to panic and feel anxious: *"Your mind is accidentally sending you danger signals when there is no real danger to fear. Let me hold your hands and as we begin to slow our breathing right down you'll quickly notice how much better you start to feel."*

STEP 5: TAPPING AFFIRMATIONS

Wanting to combine the tapping with words, we created the following affirmations:

- *I want to go to school feeling calm and relaxed.*
- *I can go to school feeling calm and relaxed.*
- *I will go to school feeling calm and relaxed.*
- *I am going to school feeling calm and relaxed.*

STEP 6: GRADUAL DESENSITISATION

We agreed that Liam was unlikely to suddenly turn around and go to school one day as if nothing had happened – he had spent too much time away from it now. I recommended a gradual re-introduction, so rather than having home visits from the teacher, Liam agreed he would be happy to go into school on Tuesday and Friday afternoons to hand in homework and pick up new assignments. Making these visits at the end of the day, rather than at the start, meant Liam often met a friend and there was an opportunity to spend some time together.

As well as avoiding school, Liam had got into the habit of missing out on other social occasions too, preferring to stay at home alone. We knew we had to change his perception that the outside world was fearful.

We identified a few more opportunities for Liam to mix with his school friends again – the swimming gala at the local pool and the school fair that took place one Saturday. His mother started inviting friends over for tea on a regular basis and he started to receive invitations in return. She admitted to me that she had stopped being proactive in engineering social situations for her son, primarily because she had found his behaviour challenging. She had struggled to get him to school and frankly was exhausted with it all. I sympathised – I regularly see parents who understandably feel worn out by such challenging situations and it can be easy to lose sight of what to do for the best. Talking the situation through with me offered an opportunity for getting clarity.

I recommended creating a 'vision board' for Liam's outings. At the centre of a large piece of board, Liam and his mother stuck a photograph of their house. I then asked them to stick photos of all the places Liam was comfortable visiting. He started off with a picture of his grandmother's house and the local supermarket – and then added his school and the events he went to as well as pictures of his friends' houses. When a friend came to visit him, he would take another photo and add this to the board too. Gradually, the board began to fill with pictures and it wasn't long before he was asking to go out, so he could add another one to the collection.

This was an important exercise as it helped Liam to change his self-image – to date, he'd got stuck in a cycle of seeing himself as a timid boy who couldn't go out anywhere. The vision board helped him to see that that was no longer true and he was changing.

STEP 7: SPINNING

Then I moved on to tackling those 'black, wriggly worms' inside Liam's tummy. I had him stand in front of me and asked him to use his index finger to point to the 'worms' and show me which way they were moving (p. 97). Sometimes, it can take a little while for children to identify the direction of movement accurately, so I had to ask Liam to become aware of this on one of his afternoon visits to the school. When he came back to see me, he was able to show me that he could sense the 'worms' were moving in an anti-clockwise direction.

I told him to put the brakes on all that movement and get them to stay still. Once they were still, I asked him to change the colour of the worms – they were black and I asked him if there was a different colour that he'd like to choose – a colour that he felt represented good feelings. He chose yellow. I asked him to close his eyes and change the colour as I snapped my fingers.

Next we needed to get the worms moving in the opposite direction – I asked him to use his index finger again to point at his tummy to get them to turn in a clockwise direction – and once we had a nice rhythm, I got Liam to speed them up a little. So now we had nice bright yellow worms travelling in the opposite direction. Liam started to laugh as he did this and I could see that we had broken through those unwanted feelings and created the shift in energy that was needed.

I finished off by asking him if he wanted to change the 'worms' for something else, because not everyone would think having worms in their tummy would be a nice experience. He surprised me when he refused but quickly explained that his worms were the sweet ones you could buy in the supermarket, so he was very happy to have them in his tummy and didn't want them taken away. We laughed at this.

STEP 8: GOING BACK TO SCHOOL

To help with the moment of separation, I told Liam's mum to start creating space between herself and him before getting to the point of parting. It's best to avoid carrying a clingy child into school and if they insist on this, find an excuse to be unable to do it, e.g. carrying bags. Let go of holding hands before the final moment – just ease off gently. Better still, try to walk in with other children and parents and insert them into the space between yourself and your child. This will make that final moment of separation much easier.

Liam's mum liaised with the school and they arranged for Liam to have a buddy/support person with him for each lesson and at lunchtime. His favourite teacher met him at the door on the first morning back and took him to his classroom which kicked things off nicely. His mum came to collect him.

I also asked Liam's mum to explain to him exactly what she would be doing with her time once she had left him. I think this is an important step as children often feel we've vanished into thin air when we leave them and not surprisingly worry that we'll never return. As well as telling him all about her work, I asked her to tell Liam that she would be thinking of him and would go to the shops to buy him a new pair of socks that he needed – on another day, I got her to say that she would be going back home and looking for the lost book that they'd been searching for the night before.

Let your child know that you are thinking of them while they're at school and that you're still 'parenting' them.

Liam was able to go to school – initially for the mornings only and a further two weeks later he came to see me again. I followed up all the exercises we had covered before and then added in this extra one:

STEP 9: IN TWO MINDS

Now that Liam had returned to school he could see that not every moment at school was nerve-wracking. He admitted that he did have good moments and did enjoy seeing his friends. He still felt slightly nervous about the prospect of spending the whole day there. On the one hand, he did want to go to school but on the other hand, he wanted to be at home, where it was safe and comfortable too.

This exercise (p. 100) helped him overcome those last feelings of doubt.

15

Bullying

The long-term effects of bullying in childhood should not be underestimated. This could be physical bullying involving harming or intimidating someone physically; verbal bullying with hurtful teasing; psychological bullying which deliberately excludes a child from their social group; and the spreading of hurtful rumours of the newest kind – that of online bullying, which results in widespread harm both emotionally and socially.

The days of thinking that bullying is 'just a part of growing up and a bit of teasing never hurt anyone' are long gone. Research carried out by King's College London in 2014[4] found that adults who experienced bullying as children, often go on to have mental health issues which hamper their relationships, earning potential and can even cause obesity.

Every school is now required to have a Bullying Policy and if you suspect your child is struggling because of another child's actions then it's wise to report it and discuss it with teachers. Quite often children will want this to be the very last thing that a parent does, but today's schools are more understanding and the days of 'telling tales' that lead to a punishment for the bully with subsequent repercussions for the bullied child are, thankfully, fading. There are more subtle ways for teachers to investigate bullying episodes and devise appropriate responses now.

If you do feel your child's school is not responding to your concerns about bullying sufficiently, it is possible to complain to Ofsted and relevant details are available online.

In Chapter 4, 'Let's talk', I recommend creating opportunities for having conversations with your child on a regular basis. If you've fallen out of the habit of having longer chats, it's going to be a lot harder for them to come to you if they have a problem. If they feel awkward or uncomfortable and they suspect that you're too busy, then they won't do it at all. Ensure you keep having regular conversations about the good things that happen in life too, rather than just problems that crop up from time to time.

In my own family discussions, I found it useful to bring up difficulties my children's friends were experiencing. We'd sympathise with their situation and talk about possible solutions and what they could have done differently to avoid the problem. Other times, I'd invent a friend's child and tell them about an imaginary problem just so we could have a chat about a possible scenario, if I felt it was needed. It makes it much easier to talk about someone else's problem rather than having your child feel as if they're being lectured by Mum or Dad.

This reminds me of the famous hypnotherapist Milton Erickson – considered by many to be the world's best. In therapy sessions with his clients, he'd often bring up a story about 'My friend John'. No-one seems to know for sure whether he did really have a friend called John, but one thing is certain, this poor man got into many scrapes and had a whole host of problems – which, of course, he successfully overcame with just the right mindset.

ISOBEL – AGE 14

Isobel's parents brought her to see me because she'd been the victim of online bullying. The trigger event had been quite benign – she'd been asked a question in class by her teacher and had given the wrong answer. Howls of laughter emanating from her classmates compounded Isobel's embarrassment. Later that evening, she discovered she was the subject of a conversation on a WhatsApp group. The incident in class was raised once more and things started to escalate. Her classmates decided it would be 'fun' to keep taunting her.

After a couple of days, the conversation died down and Isobel felt relieved that it was over. However, the silence didn't last for too long and when it resurfaced, the bullying comments started to multiply. After a few more days, the original incident of not being able to answer the question in class had been forgotten, but there were two girls who continued to send her nasty messages online.

Fortunately, Isobel's parents realised something was making her unhappy and when they discovered the reason, had a chat with her teachers. While the matter was being handled well by the school, Isobel had become jumpy and nervous. She felt as if 'everyone' was looking at and making fun of her and she started to avoid after-school events and decline party invitations from friends 'just in case'.

As I explained earlier, our minds are programmed to make generalisations, so just as a bad encounter with *one* dog can easily create a phobia of *all* dogs, in much the same way, being teased or bullied at school by one or two people can send your child's mind into overdrive and a state of hypervigilance. It's natural to feel that 'everyone' is out to get them and 'no-one' (in the entire world) likes them and that they don't have any friends at all.

I explained to Isobel's parents that it's important to recognise that she wasn't exaggerating or making this up – she will be genuinely feeling as if this is all true. Simply telling a child that things are not how they see them isn't usually enough to change their thinking – this has to be more subtle, and positive steps need to be taken on a more long-term basis.

During my conversations with Isobel, I was able to establish that because the nasty comments had appeared on her mobile phone, each time she picked it up she felt as if she was carrying the bullies around with her. She told me that *"They're living in my school bag . . . They're in my phone . . Each time I hold my phone I feel like their comments are sinking into my hands . . .".*

She also told me that she couldn't stop feeling stupid for having got the answer wrong in class in the first place.

STEP 1: TFT – TAPPING TECHNIQUE

I often like using the Tapping technique (p. 77) in the initial instance. If I have a child in front of me that is crying and struggling to tell their story, then clearing the energy space by tapping helps to restore some balance. It's usual to give off a couple of deep sighs after a tapping routine and when I see this happen, I know we can proceed to the next step.

STEP 2: DELETING UNWANTED IMAGES AND INTERNAL DIALOGUE

I knew Isobel would start to feel better if we could deal with the persistent images she had in her mind of those messages – and also the nasty voices that had become a part of her internal dialogue. Research shows that it's easier to brush off and forget a nasty comment that's spoken to us, whereas hurtful remarks that are written down for us to read will hurt more and be harder to dismiss.

We ran through the Magic TV Control exercise (p. 86) and the Volume Control exercise (p. 91).

STEP 3: BUILDING RESILIENCE

We know that children who give off an air of quiet assured confidence are less likely to be bullied and I explained to Isobel's parents that there are several things they could be doing at home to support her in order to help her become more emotionally resilient. Chapter 9 on general worrying gives details on how to tackle negative thinking and encourage more positive thoughts. Doing this each day will help Isobel to develop good habits and stop seeing herself as so 'stupid' – and in turn, make her less of a bully's target.

STEP 4: CONFIDENCE ANCHOR

It was time to help Isobel remember that whilst she may have made one tiny mistake by not knowing the correct answer in class, this in fact was not who or what she was.

I helped her set up a confidence anchor (p. 104) so that in the future she could use this whenever she needs to feel more confident and stronger in herself. She can use it the night before school if she's feeling worried about the next day or she can use it when she's actually at school and anxious that someone might pick on her.

In order to get that flow of feelgood chemicals in her body, I asked her to think of three times in the past when she felt really good.

- The first special moment I anchored was the memory she had of the family holiday to Disneyland last year – this was one of the best moments in her life as she had wanted to visit for so long.

- The second moment we anchored was a time when she just couldn't stop laughing with her friends. Often the funniest moments are when we really shouldn't be laughing and our attempts to suppress the laughter just make the situation all the funnier. She chose a time when she was sitting in a maths class and her teacher spilt her cup of coffee all over the table. As she told me this story, she started to laugh again and this was perfect for me as I knew it was just the right time to anchor those feelings.

- The third moment was one where a teacher had praised her work. I encouraged her to search through her memory bank as I was sure there would have been a time like this. She chose the time she and her friend had come top in the class for a geography project. I especially wanted her to choose a moment where she had done well at school as this would counter-balance the original incident of getting the answer wrong.

STEP 5: GUIDED VISUALISATION

As always, I wanted to leave Isobel with a good, positive picture in her mind to fill the empty space left by the old images. After an initial relaxation with her eyes closed, I asked Isobel to imagine herself somewhere nice: she chose her local park – there was a big tree there that she liked to sit under with her friends. I got her to imagine herself there again and to notice what she could see, hear and feel.

She said that she could **see** people playing tennis on the courts in the corner of the park; she could **hear** the leaves of the oak tree rustling as the branches swayed in the wind and she could also **feel** the soft mossy grass bank that she was sitting on.

Then I asked her to list six people that she knows love and adore her. She chose her sister, mother, two school friends, her good friend who lives next door and because she felt stuck at this point, I told her she could choose the family pet dog – Dante.

I asked her to imagine them all sitting around the oak tree in a circle with herself in the middle up against the tree trunk. I asked her to look around the circle of friends and one by one imagine what they would want to say to her if they really knew how miserable all the bullies at school had made her. Up until this moment, she hadn't discussed anything with these friends; only her mother and sister knew what she had been through. She closed her eyes and imagined each person looking at her with affection as one-by-one they gave her a lovely, supportive message.

After a few moments, I asked Isobel to tell me how that experience had been for her. She had tears in her eyes as she told me that all of them had said that they loved her (including the dog!) and that three of them had said they were shocked that she had kept this to herself for so long and were sad for her and sad too they had not been there to help her. This experience helped her to gain perspective – yes, there were one or two people at school who disliked her but there were so many more people around her who loved and cared for her.

Capitalising on this experience, I asked Isobel to close her eyes once more and create a picture in her imagination of her mobile phone. This time rather than seeing nasty messages from the school bullies, I asked her to create messages from her friends and family using the words that had come up during this imaginary conversation with them as she sat under the tree.

STEP 6: FUTURE PACE

In the background, Isobel's parents had been liaising with teachers and things were starting to resolve themselves at school. New lessons had been introduced advising pupils on the rules around posting messages online and what was acceptable and what was not. And sanctions were quickly introduced for those who did not follow the guidelines.

Isobel started to feel a lot better – as she told me, she simply felt as if the 'heat' had been taken out of the situation. She no longer felt so upset and had started to sleep better.

I did a final visualisation exercise with her: I asked her to see herself going to school – having asked for the relevant details about her journey, I was able to guide her through the usual steps that she took. Then, once at school, I had her see everything go just the way she would want it to. So the first positive thing that happened was her best friend was waiting by the school gate and they were able to walk in together. I guided her through this imaginary day and had her successfully navigate her way around school without seeing the bullies.

She could see her friends and I got her to 'step out of the image' and see herself (dissociate) and notice the expression on her face. Isobel could see herself happy and smiling. Then I asked her to slip back into the image, become associated once more and feel how good this feels.

16

Exam stress

Exams frighten most of us and today's students have to face more of them than previous generations, so it's not surprising that stress and anxiety can begin to overwhelm even the most able. Feelings of nervousness can quickly lead to a lack of motivation to study and underperformance regardless of academic potential and ability.

As parents we have an instinctive urge to keep our children safe and out of harm's way. Watching them struggle with one of life's biggest challenges independently, can be very frustrating. Some parents have overwhelming desires to 'do something' to help, but remember, a gentle prod can be helpful but a shove rarely is. It's time to play a more supportive role.

While there's no substitute for real knowledge acquired throughout the academic year, there are other little things that can make all the difference between success and failure. Preparation is the key to success and here's some advice I feel is useful:

1. **Choose revision surroundings carefully:** The more these match the exam room environment, the better. Lying on a bed or sitting in the garden under a tree may seem like a nice idea to make those hours of studying easier, but sitting at a table will help your child's body associate this position with their studies. Recalling the information in exam conditions will be a lot easier when they adopt a similar pose.

2. **Can your child see?** In Chapter 2, I explained how our mind automatically makes images from our thoughts and being able to notice these will help your child to remember content

and come up with correct answers. Some of us get a sense that our mental images are inside our head and others will feel as if they're far out in the distance or even perhaps above on the ceiling. For this reason, I would advocate positioning a desk in front of a window rather than up against a wall as this will help your child to 'see' and think more clearly.

3. **Junk food, junk mind:** Children need to be eating well throughout this stressful time, for if you want your mind and body to be working at its best, you need to think about the fuel that is being put into it. I remember receiving advice from one of my children's schools telling us that it's fine for them to be eating junk food at this time if that's their choosing. I don't really agree with this. The exam period could last up to 8 weeks and eating nutritionally deficient foods for that length of time will not help them to pass. If your child's most difficult maths paper happens to be right at the end of the 8-week period, then having gorged on sugary snacks and sweets all that time is not going to help them feel calm and to concentrate easily. Remember what I mentioned earlier about sugary foods creating feelings of anxiety.

4. **Get moving:** If your child shows clear signs of feeling grumpy or fed up with revision, ensure they're taking regular breaks that enable them to move around to get their circulation and energy flow moving in a better way – this will make it harder for the body to hang onto negative feelings. Taking a break to play a computer game is more likely to add to feelings of anxiety rather than take them away. Studies show that children who do aerobic exercise such as cycling, swimming, playing football and running achieve higher exam results.

5. **Sleep:** Ensure your child gets plenty of sleep and, within reason, sticks to their usual waking and sleeping hours. It's best not to slip into holiday mode during study leave for it makes getting up for exams that much harder. This is especially important if they have an afternoon exam – it's important to get up at their usual morning waking time in order to be in the best frame of mind

WHAT KIND OF LEARNER IS YOUR CHILD?

We use all our senses to absorb information from our environment and our senses form the basis of our learning preference or style. Taking a few moments to observe your child to figure out which methods suit them best may help avoid a whole lot of homework angst.

Your child may favour any of the following learning styles:

- **Visual**. These children prefer to learn by seeing information. They like reading, pictures or diagrams, demonstrations and watching videos. Eventually they'll picture the information in their minds.

- **Auditory**. Here they prefer to learn by hearing or saying it. They enjoy listening to audio downloads, podcasts, lectures, debates, discussions and verbal instructions. They may ask you to repeat a set of instructions over and over again: they like hearing it being said.

- **Kinaesthetic**. Children with this preference learn best by getting a feel for it. They enjoy physical involvement, hands-on work, moving around and touching.

Lynn O'Brien of Specific Diagnostic Studies Inc, found that about 40% of people have a preference for a visual learning style, 15% for auditory and 45% for kinaesthetic.[5]

If you can determine your child's preferred learning style you'll be able to adapt any homework activity to suit them better.

BE AWARE OF WHAT WORKS BEST

Everyone is different, so help your child figure out what does and does not work well for them. If they tell you they had a particularly good revision session, make a note of the details such as the time of day, the location, whether it was totally quiet or with background noise. Note whether they'd just eaten and notice the particular book or system that they were using. If it worked well on one occasion, the chances are it will work well again.

Work with your child to help them begin noticing how different revision styles suit different people. They may get on better:

- recording their voice on a Dictaphone or perhaps on a mobile phone;
- using a whiteboard and coloured pens to group information;
- creating flash cards;
- using rhymes, mnemonics or mind maps; or
- having someone to test them.

Looking at 2 years' worth of geography files can feel slightly daunting for anyone. Chunking it down into smaller sections and categories will make it easier to remember.

KIARA – AGE 17

When Kiara came to see me, she was clearly struggling with her final year at school. She was having problems sleeping at night and her skin had broken out in angry, red rashes.

In previous years, she had experienced bouts of the usual exam nerves, but this year in particular there was far more going on. She'd applied to university and was worried about whether she'd get the right grades to go to her first choice. On the one hand she was looking forward to going to uni, but on the other hand her mind was full of worries:

- Would she actually like her new uni?
- Would she be able to make new friends easily?
- What if she didn't like the course she had chosen?
- What about money? There were the tuition fees to consider and she didn't like the idea of taking out loans and getting into debt.

By definition a new beginning means something has to end and while the prospect of leaving home was exciting, Kiara was sad about leaving school and all her friends, as well as her familiar home surroundings, her younger sister and their Labrador Jess.

All of these feelings were flooding her brain with too many stress chemicals.

We know that having a positive mental attitude will help with concentration and memory but simply telling someone to *"try to stay positive"* is unlikely to do the trick. And do remember what I said about using the word *'try'* in the 'Words that Work' section in Chapter 4 – it can make things worse.

There were a few therapeutic exercises that I knew would help Kiara to stay calm and focused.

STEP 1: OVERCOMING DOUBTS

On the one hand Kiara was really excited about going to university but on the other hand she was naturally worried. I showed her how to work through the 'In two minds' exercise (p. 100). Each of us has an internal dialogue and this can be made up of many different voices. As much as we might try to think positive thoughts, there's very often a negative dialogue going on in the background too. I explained to Kiara that rather than wishing to sabotage her attempts to successfully pass her exams and go to university, the negative voice was simply showing concern – it was trying to keep her safe and look out for her.

This exercise is a useful way of letting that negative voice or that concerned 'part' of you know that you've received the message it is sending to you – and that you have solutions to potential problems already in mind. It's usual to find that the negative part of you begins to calm down after this exercise.

STEP 2: STOP THAT THOUGHT

I showed Kiara another useful exercise for dealing with the negative thoughts that creep into our minds just when we don't need them. I used the 'Stop that thought' exercise (p. 94). I reminded her that we have lots of thoughts rushing through our minds each and every day and most of them we take no notice of whatsoever. They pop up and we simply let them float away. We can choose whether or not to engage with them – it happens naturally. Kiara laughed and agreed that a little thought telling her to sort out her overflowing laundry basket often popped into her mind but she kept dismissing it, much to her mother's annoyance.

I told her that as she already knew how to despatch unwanted thoughts very effectively, with a little bit of practice she'd be able to handle her negative ones too.

STEP 3: CREATE A BRIGHT, NEW, SHINY FUTURE

Quite often when we face a hurdle in life, our ability to see over the other side of it becomes diminished. How can you imagine a wonderful life at university, when you have a set of difficult exams to get through first? In just the same way, it can be hard to feel excited about an upcoming holiday if you have an intense fear of flying. We start to feel stuck and the more we focus on the challenge ahead of us, the more anxious we start to feel.

I guided Kiara through the 'Bright, new, shiny future' exercise (p. 110). It's not always easy to imagine yourself at an event in the future if you've never experienced it before. How can you possibly know what to expect? But this can work to our advantage too, because as I took her through this exercise, she was able to dream, imagine and invent whatever details she hoped to have in her new life at university. She saw herself with lots of new friends, nice lodgings and friendly tutors. When we discussed what she saw for herself in her future life, she told me that the sun always seemed to be shining and interestingly, she was wearing some lovely new clothes too.

Seeing yourself at a time in the future with everything going just the way you'd like it to go is a great way of taking the heat or the sting out of an immediately stressful situation. Picture yourself *after* the event and you'll start to feel better straightaway.

Kiara left the session feeling very much calmer. As well as recommending that she repeat these exercises again at home, I also introduced her to the self-soothing Havening Techniques (p. 83).

17

Travel anxiety

Fear of flying

Holidays are supposed to be fun, relaxing and a special treat to look forward to. So many of us, though, find that packing up to leave our jobs, homes, family pets and usual routines can be stressful.

Thoughts of relaxing, sunny beaches and exciting new experiences can quickly turn into worries about strange foods, illnesses, a shortage of money, never mind all the fears of travelling by air, sea and driving on strange roads (in less than road-worthy vehicles). These feelings of stress and anxiety leave many of us wondering whether it's actually worth it.

And if you have a child that suffers from travel anxiety, this can quickly escalate the whole experience into a nightmare for everyone in the family.

XAVIER – AGE 7

Xavier's parents brought him to see me because they were off on a long-haul trip to Florida at Christmas. Although they travelled regularly as a family, all their holidays involved going back home to visit family in France. Xavier was used to travelling on the Eurostar train and also on cross-channel ferries but had never flown in an aeroplane. His anxiety stemmed from seeing a plane crash on a TV news report some six months ago. It had been hard to shield him from all the details as it was heavily covered by the media at the time.

STEP 1: DEALING WITH WORRIES

I encouraged Xavier's parents to create a Worry Box (p. 118). We knew that his parents would not be able to address all their son's worries about the upcoming trip. After all, how can you hand on heart assure your child that the plane you'll be travelling on won't crash? None of us has a crystal ball but so many of us take this risk simply because we know it's one worth taking. The chances of being involved in an air disaster are miniscule – tiny, in fact. We are all far more likely to lose our lives crossing the street and yet we do this each and every day quite happily. But if you explain this to a child, they may well develop a fear of going out of the house so this needs careful handling.

I recommended the Worry Box because I knew that if Xavier was working himself up about the upcoming holiday, his anxiety would also be spilling over into other areas of his life. Xavier was encouraged to write each of his worries down on a piece of paper as and when they cropped up and then post them into the Worry Box. Each week he sat down with his parents and went through them one by one. His worries varied from failing to remember the correct spellings for a test at school to worrying about having no-one to talk to at his friend's birthday party. Gradually he started to see 'proof and evidence' that most of the things we worry about turn out to be OK in the end and that you don't always need to know every detail about something that's going to happen in the future in order to feel calm and relaxed about it.

STEP 2: VISION BOARD

I asked Xavier's parents to start filling in all the details about the holiday. To date, the focus had been on the flight and conversations rarely got beyond this stage.

They'd told Xavier that they'd be going on holiday, but what does that look like exactly? I encouraged them to spend some time explaining where they would be going and to cut pictures of the resort out of holiday brochures or to print them off the internet to create a 'vision board'. I asked them to add in as many details as possible including places that they planned to visit and in particular to find pictures of other children enjoying the resort as this would make it easier for Xavier to imagine himself there. We fear the unknown and making this new experience more real will dilute the anxiety. The vision board was placed in Xavier's bedroom so he could look at it each evening.

STEP 3: VISUALISATION TECHNIQUES

When I worked with Xavier, I asked him to think about where the worrying thought about flying in that holiday plane had come from. He was able to clearly remember the news item on TV that had triggered it all off.

I asked him to describe the thought – what could he see and what could he hear? I introduced him to the Magic TV Control (p. 86) and also the Volume Control (p. 91). Remember that changing the pictures and sounds in the imagination will change the way a person feels.

It became clear that there was more than one version of this scary image in his mind, which was not surprising because the news item had been reported many times over on TV and he'd also seen pictures in the newspapers. It's important to remember that each of these images or episodes should be dealt with separately. One of the images that had particularly upset him was one where relatives were filmed looking distraught at the airport once they'd heard the bad news about their loved ones.

It's possible to be creative with visualisation techniques and it's not necessary to use exactly the same solution each time to eradicate the image. To deal with one of the particularly distressing images, I chatted with Xavier to see what he thought would be effective. Together we came up with the idea of holding a pot of white paint and a huge paintbrush. He then dipped the brush into the paint and painted all over the image, whitening it out completely.

To deal with the sounds that accompanied that picture, I had Xavier imagine playing a favourite piece of music really loudly as he painted to drown the sounds out.

If your child struggles to do this inside their imagination, you can ask them to draw the scary thoughts on a piece of paper and then to erase them - they can either paint over them or tear the piece of paper up into tiny pieces and throw them all away.

Once the image was gone completely, Xavier was able to put a better picture in its place – one that he had on his vision board. He chose a favourite: one of a few children sliding down a slide into a swimming pool.

STEP 4: DESENSITISATION

Next, I suggested that Xavier's parents should take steps to gradually desensitise his fear of flying by visiting an airport. Here they could watch planes take off and land, spend time sitting in one of the coffee shops and choose some interesting books and games for the flight itself. I told them to remember to also visit the toilets as worrying about these is often a cause of anxiety, then to explain exactly what will happen when the family arrives to go on the trip and also to point out all the people who are there to help us. Uniformed security staff, especially those with weapons, can look scary, so it's good to explain that they look after us and keep us safe.

To finish off I suggested they take photos or a video on a phone so that Xavier could use these to describe what he did and saw at the airport to other family members or friends.

STEP 5: TFT – TAPPING TECHNIQUE

I recommended that the family all learn how to use the TFT Tapping technique (p. 77) and practise it on a regular basis. I usually recommend each evening for a week before going on holiday as this will detox the feelings of anxiety that often get mixed in with feelings of excitement before a big event.

It's a good handy technique to use at the airport and also on the plane. This technique is now so well known for travel anxiety that I'd be very surprised if there isn't another passenger on your plane also using it. There are short-cuts that you can use when you're in public places – tapping under the eye and also tapping on the side of the hand so there's no need to feel self-conscious about doing it. Do make use of the affirmations with your tapping too, e.g. *"I want to feel calm and relaxed as I travel on the plane."*

Note: I also recommend that children learn a breathing technique (p. 65) such as pretending to blow up a balloon by blowing out slowly and deeply into their scrunched up hand. This will come in handy if for some reason you need a quick and easy option should a problem occur. For anxious travellers, it's also useful to have some hypnosis and relaxation downloads to listen to while travelling.

18

Sleep problems

Sleep problems in children can leave the whole family feeling exhausted and I often meet parents who tell me they're up and down several times in the night having to attend to their child's woes. Often this is a problem that's been going on for many years and that in itself adds to the challenge, as having become an established pattern of behaviour it's likely your child won't remember acting differently.

Studies show that sleep deprivation is a major cause of anxiety, which is interesting, because anxiety is usually the reason why someone can't sleep! A lack of sleep will also affect your child's academic performance and general behaviour as well as cause food cravings and obesity. So finding solutions to sleep problems is very important.

In this chapter I'm going to explain how to help a child that wakes with nightmares or a fear of 'something under the bed'. You can find more solutions for dealing with bedtime problems, including separation anxiety, in my other book *Words that Work*. If you're one of the many parents who have to sit by their child's side until they fall asleep, you'll find advice in here that will help you.

ESTABLISH A GOOD ROUTINE AND STICK TO IT

I know how tempting it can be to allow a child who's nervous about going to sleep, to spend some time unwinding and snoozing on the downstairs sofa until you can easily transfer them into bed, but this could be making your child's problem worse. They'll find it increasingly difficult to get into the habit of falling asleep independently and you'll be forever stuck with them on the sofa. It's important to learn how to lie in bed and fall asleep naturally

We've all fallen asleep in front of the TV, only to wake up feeling disorientated and then struggle to get to sleep when we do actually go to bed. It disrupts the pattern of our sleep cycle and if this regularly happens to your child it only adds to your bedtime troubles.

Decide on a regular bed time and stick to the same routine each day.

KEEP THE BEDROOM TIDY

It's not relaxing for a child to sleep in a room that has dirty clothes, toys, books and shoes strewn all over the floor. We all feel calmer in an uncluttered environment and the tidying up process can become an automatic part of the bedtime routine. It's something you'll be able to do together and will signal the 'end of the day'.

IS THE ROOM TOO LIGHT?

It's better to sleep in a dark environment because light and hormones dictate our sleep patterns. When light dims in the evening, we produce a chemical called melatonin, which gives the body clock its cue that it's time to sleep. The sooner you can train your child to sleep in a dark room so much the better. There's a trend to have night-lights on in bedrooms to help children fall asleep but I recommend weaning your child off these as soon as you can, by taking small steps to making the room darker each night until you remove the light completely. It is possible to buy night-lights that are fitted with a motion-sensor – the light will automatically come on as soon as it detects someone is moving about in the room. This may be an ideal compromise for you.

AVOID ELECTRONIC GADGETS

Having items like mobile phones, laptops and iPads recharging near the bed is not a good idea, for the electro magnetic field created by these stimulates the mind and will keep your child awake. And, if they're awake in the small hours of the morning, the temptation to go on to social media and chat to friends will be too great if the phone is under the pillow. Likewise, it's better not to have TVs and DVD players in the room; bedrooms are for sleeping and relaxing in. This may be tough for your child but it's important for good health.

WORDS THAT WORK: PUT IT IN THE PAST

Start talking about the problem as if your child is already starting to get over it, like so:

- *You used to really struggle to fall asleep but I'm noticing that as each day passes it's getting a little easier for you. You're probably starting to notice this too, aren't you?*
- *You often used to wake in the night feeling really scared but I can see that it's happening less now – it shows you're beginning to grow out of it.*

Even if things haven't started to change, your child will respond more favourably to these positive words and start moving in the right direction. Remember how I explained that pictures or mental images are created in our minds by the words that we hear spoken around us. Calm soothing words create good pictures which create good feelings.

EMILIE – AGE 11

Emilie's parents brought her to see me because she was becoming increasingly distressed when trying to sleep, saying she felt there was 'something under the bed'. This usually happened around 10pm when her parents were still up watching TV downstairs. She would come running down to see them in a panic with her heart racing and her skin clammy.

I've already mentioned how common this fear is and it's worth repeating – an American study found that 87% of people have a fear of sleeping with their feet sticking out of the covers just in case they get eaten up. So she's not alone!

Once Emilie was up and out of bed it was often a struggle to get her back in. One of her parents would need to sit with her until she fell asleep again and occasionally they would let her stay up for a glass of milk and a biscuit.

It was easy to see that these solutions were creating 'secondary gains' for Emilie but I wasn't convinced that this was the reason why she was waking in a panic.

STEP 1: KEEPING A DIARY

I started by asking for more information about Emilie's daily routine, including what she was eating. It transpired that on two nights of the week, she had after school swimming sessions, which meant she was coming home late and often ate a couple of sandwiches in the car on the way home.

I asked her parents to start keeping a diary to record her daily activities, including her diet and also the nights when she was waking in a panic. I advised them to start acting a little like a detective and to ask themselves the question *"What did Emilie do and what did she eat in the previous 24 hours?"* each time she had a bad episode in the evening.

STEP 2 TFT – TAPPING TECHNIQUE

I showed them how to use the Tapping technique on (p. 77) and we used it as she was thinking about the creature under her bed. I then recommended that they use it with Emilie each morning and evening for at least a week. In the evenings she could combine the tapping with affirmations. She chose the words *'I want to feel happy, calm and relaxed when I'm sleeping in my bed'*. And then followed it up with another round using the words *'I want to sleep soundly till morning time'*.

STEP 3: VISUALISATION TECHNIQUE

I taught Emilie how to change those scary thoughts. She could clearly describe what the *'something under the bed'* looked like. It was like a green monster with spikey bits on the top of his head and fangs for teeth. Using the Magic TV Control exercise (p. 86) she changed the intensity of the image by draining the colours out so it became black and white. Then quite suddenly she declared that she wanted to squash it flat – as flat as a piece of paper. And after doing this, she decided to fold it in half – and then in half again.

I asked her what she wanted to do next and she wasn't sure. So I gave her some options and she chose to imagine writing 'Return to Sender' on this flat piece of paper and taking it to the post office and posting it in the letter box. She wanted to get rid of this monster but at the same time, didn't want to cause it a great deal of harm.

I asked her to close her eyes and did a guided visualisation exercise with her, so she could see herself doing this. She felt very happy with the outcome and I told Emilie that if ever the creature came back into her thoughts at night-time, she now knew exactly what she needed to do – drain out the colours, squash it flat and take it to the post office.

Within a couple of weeks, Emilie proved to be a much calmer sleeper. The regular tapping was reducing her anxiety levels and simply knowing that she had a strategy in place should the monster under the bed return, meant that it rarely did.

By keeping a regular diary, Emilie's parents were able to see that there was a connection between her restless nights and the after-school swimming sessions. She was coming home quite hyped up, and wolfing down those late evening sandwiches in the car wasn't helping either.

I showed them how to use the Havening Techniques (p. 83) and recommended that they do this together each evening at bedtime to help Emilie relax more easily. She was quickly able to learn this self-soothing exercise and if ever she woke in the night, she would do this rather than calling out for Mum and Dad. Everyone was able to sleep better as a result.

Note: Another option would be to ask your child to draw a picture of the monster and then change the way it looks by drawing over it, using different colours and adding details to it – a nice, happy smile perhaps or something that makes it look comical. Emilie's monster wasn't making any sounds but if it had been, I would also have encouraged her to use the Volume Control technique (p. 91).

Some children might 'feel' as if there is a monster under the bed but have no visual or auditory cues so using the Magic TV Control wouldn't be appropriate. In this instance, I would ask where inside their body they were feeling the scary feelings and use the Spinning technique (p. 97).

Another option is to ask your child if they would like an imaginary guard to stand by the side of the bed to ensure the monster doesn't return. Favourite super-heroes, TV characters and family pets are good options. Remember, this is an imaginary exercise – you won't really need to park the family Labrador by the side of your child's bed each evening!

A final note

I do hope you've found the information in this book helpful and that you'll be able to implement many of the strategies into your daily lives from now on. Introducing good, positive thinking patterns, sooner rather than later, will help your child learn how to stay emotionally healthy. The benefits of this will be felt not just in the immediate future but throughout the course of their life, so it will be worth it.

I know the phrase 'every child is different' can be such an annoying thing for a parent to hear – how convenient would it be if there were a 'one-size fits all, quick fix'. Not every technique will work with every child so please don't lose heart if something doesn't work the first time. It's possible to play around and experiment with the techniques, modifying them to suit your needs and I hope this book will have given you plenty of ideas on how you can do just that.

As the title of this book suggests, the information here should be regarded as 'First Aid'. Of course, you may find this is the only aid you need to help your child overcome their anxiety but if you do feel that you're struggling, please do seek out help from a suitably qualified practitioner. There are many good people out there who can help you.

With my very best wishes,

Alicia

Notes

1. For more information see: www.nspcc.org.uk/what-we-do/
    news-opinion/one-third-increase-in-school-referrals-for-
    mental-health-treatment/.

2. National Association of Sleep Comfort and Coziness (NASCC),
    see http://empirenews.net/87-of-population-fear-having-feet-
    grabbed-by-boogeyman-if-left-uncovered-during-sleep/

3. See www.hsj.gr/medicine/impact-of-a-singlesession-of-
    havening.php?aid=7273.

4. See www.kcl.ac.uk/ioppn/news/records/2014/April/Impact-
    of-childhood-bullying-still-evident-after-40-years

5. Dee Dickinson (2002). *Learning Through the Arts: New Horizons
    for Learning*. https://pa01000192.schoolwires.net/cms/lib/
    PA01000192/Centricity/Domain/162/Learning_Through_the_
    Arts.pdf.

Useful contact details

YOUNG MINDS
The UK's leading charity for children and young people's mental health.
Parents Helpline: 0808 802 5544
For urgent help text YM to 85258
www.youngminds.org.uk

CHILDLINE
A free and confidential advice service for children.
0800 1111
www.childline.org.uk

NSPCC
Offers help and advice for adults concerned about a child.
0808 800 5000
www.nspcc.org.uk

CAMHS
Child and Adolescent Mental Health Services run by the NHS. Ask your GP or local hospital for further details.

CHILD BEREAVEMENT UK
Offers support for families and educates professionals when a baby or child of any age dies or is dying, and when a child is facing bereavement.
www.childbereavement.org.uk

HEADS TOGETHER
Heads Together is a mental health initiative spearheaded by The Royal Foundation of The Duke and Duchess of Cambridge and The Duke and Duchess of Sussex, which combines a campaign to

tackle stigma and change the conversation on mental health with fundraising for a series of innovative new mental health services. www.headstogether.org.uk

GENERAL HYPNOTHERAPY STANDARDS COUNCIL (GHSC)
The GHSC and General Hypnotherapy Register (GHR) are the UK's largest and most prominent organisations within the field of hypnotherapy. You can find a register of practising hypnotherapists at: www.general-hypnotherapy-register.com

CONTEMPORARY COLLEGE OF THERAPEUTIC STUDIES
Provides validated integrated psychotherapy, practical hypnotherapy and counselling training courses in London. www.contemporarycollege.com

NLP LIFE TRAINING
Provides a range of training courses and seminars in Neuro-Linguistic Programming (NLP) for use in therapeutics, personal, coaching and corporate contexts. www.nlplifetraining.com

HAVENING TECHNIQUES
You'll find further information about the methodology, trainings and practitioners here. www.havening.org

THOUGHT FIELD THERAPY (TFT)
You can find out more about the TFT tapping technique on the creator's website. www.rogercallahan.com

MONTESSORI SOCIETY AMI
The Montessori Society is affiliated to the Association Montessori Internationale (AMI) and aims to inform teachers and parents about Montessori and its practice. www.montessorisociety.org.uk

EMPOWERING LEARNING
To find out more about the link between mental imagery and learning difficulties, I highly recommend the work of Olive Hickmott. www.empoweringlearning.co.uk

Also by Alicia Eaton

Books:
Stop Bedwetting in 7 Days (3rd Edition: Practical Inspiration 2019)

Words that Work: How to get kids to do almost anything (Matador 2015)

Fix your Life with NLP (Simon & Schuster 2012)

Audio downloads:
Dry Beds Now
Stop Bedwetting Now
A Magic Day Out
The Sleepyhead Garden
Fussy Eating No More
Stop Thumbsucking Now
Exam Success
Relax Now
Boost your Confidence
Sleep Soundly
Garden of your Life
Weight off your Mind
Hypnotic Gastric Band
Smoke Free

About the author

Originally an AMI *Montessori Teacher* Alicia ran her own school for five years and followed this up with further training and studies at the *Anna Freud Centre* in London. In 2003 she went on to train as an *Integrative Psychotherapist using Clinical Hypnotherapy* and followed this up with numerous trainings in *NLP* with Paul McKenna and assisted him with his seminars for many years. She's now a qualified *Trainer* running workshops on a variety of topics, including parenting. Over the years, she's continued to add to her skill set with trainings in *Thought Field Therapy (TFT or Tapping); Havening Techniques; Mindfulness* at the Oxford Mindfulness Centre; and *Childhood Obesity* at the National Centre for Eating Disorders.

Alicia has run a successful practice in London's Harley Street since 2004 and her unique blend of psychology and practical parenting advice means she's often the number one choice for parents seeking help with behavioural change and emotional wellbeing. From anxiety, fears and phobias to fussy eating, thumb-sucking, nail-biting, bedwetting and sleep problems, Alicia helps parents to steer their children on the right path. Alicia's work is regularly featured in the media including BBC radio, The Telegraph, Daily Mail, The Sun, Mother & Baby, Fox News, 9Jumpin'.

Her books have proved popular for their 'easy-to-read' style and the fast results that can be achieved.